KW-325-838

ENGLISH LYRICS
FROM SPENSER TO MILTON

Also in the Endymion Series

POEMS BY JOHN KEATS
Illustrated and decorated by
Robert Anning Bell

THE POEMS OF EDGAR ALLAN POE
Illustrated and decorated by
W. Heath Robinson

POEMS BY PERCY BYSSHE SHELLEY
Illustrated and decorated by
Robert Anning Bell

ENGLISH LYRICS FROM SPENSER TO MILTON

ILLUSTRATIONS BY ROBERT ANNING BELL

BELL & HYMAN
LONDON

Published by
BELL & HYMAN LIMITED
Denmark House
37-39 Queen Elizabeth Street
London SE1 2QB

First published in 1898 by
G. Bell & Sons Ltd

This edition

ISBN 0 7135 1107 9

Printed and bound in Great Britain by
Redwood Burn Limited
Trowbridge & Esher

INTRODUCTION

Robert Anning Bell is best known for his large scale works in mosaic and stained glass, undertaken during the 1920s. These large scale compositions might at first sight seem to have little in common with the delicate line drawings in the present book; but both his more formal later work and the carefree line of these earlier drawings are based on a deep love and knowledge of Renaissance style, with its softer remodelling of the forms of classical art.

Most of Anning Bell's book illustrations were completed before the First World War. His subsequent career was largely in the domain of academic and public art. He became R.A. in 1922, and was a Professor first at Liverpool then at the Royal College of Art and finally the Glasgow School of Art. His mastery of different techniques was impressive; besides the media already mentioned he was a member of the Royal Water Colour Society, frequently showed oil paintings at the Royal Academy and evolved a method of painting relief, plaster in low relief which was then coloured and gilded. He died in 1933, aged seventy.

HARK, HARK! THE LARK

W. SHAKESPEARE

HARK, hark! the lark at heaven's gate sings,
   And Phœbus 'gins arise,
His steeds to water at those springs
   On chaliced flowers that lies;
And winking Mary-buds begin
   To ope their golden eyes:
With everything that pretty is,
   My lady sweet, arise:
      Arise, arise.

LOVE'S EMBLEMS

J. FLETCHER

Now the lusty spring is seen;
  Golden yellow, gaudy blue,
  Daintily invite the view:
Everywhere on every green
Roses blushing as they blow,
  And enticing men to pull,
Lilies whiter than the snow,
  Woodbines of sweet honey full:
    All love's emblems, and all cry,
    "Ladies, if not plucked, we die."

Yet the lusty spring hath stayed;
  Blushing red and purest white
  Daintily to love invite
Every woman, every maid:
Cherries kissing as they grow,
  And inviting men to taste,
Apples even ripe below,
  Winding gently to the waist:
    All love's emblems, and all cry
    "Ladies, if not plucked, we die."

ENGLISH LYRICS

CORINNA'S MAYING

R. HERRICK

GET up, get up for shame! The blooming morn
Upon her wings presents the god unshorn.
See how Aurora throws her fair
Fresh-quilted colours through the air:
Get up, sweet Slug-a-bed, and see
The dew-bespangling herb and tree!
Each flower has wept and bowed towárd the east,
Above an hour since, yet you not drest;
Nay! not so much as out of bed;
When all the birds have matins said,
And sung their thankful hymns, 'tis sin,
Nay, profanation, to keep in,
Whenas a thousand virgins on this day
Spring, sooner than the lark, to fetch in May.

Rise, and put on your foliage, and be seen
To come forth, like the Spring-time, fresh and green,
And sweet as Flora. Take no care
For jewels for your gown or hair:
Fear not; the leaves will strew
Gems in abundance upon you:
Besides, the childhood of the day has kept,
Against you come, some orient pearls unwept.
Come, and receive them while the light
Hangs on the dew-locks of the night,
And Titan on the eastern hill
Retires himself, or else stands still
Till you come forth! Wash, dress, be brief in praying:
Few beads are best when once we go a-Maying.

Come, my Corinna, come; and coming, mark
How each field turns a street, each street a park
Made green and trimmed with trees! see how
Devotion gives each house a bough
Or branch: Each porch, each door, ere this,
An ark, a tabernacle is,

Made up of white-thorn neatly interwove,
As if here were those cooler shades of love.
Can such delights be in the street
And open fields, and we not see 't?
Come, we 'll abroad: and let 's obey
The proclamation made for May,
And sin no more, as we have done, by staying,
But, my Corinna, come, let 's go a-Maying.

There 's not a budding boy or girl this day
But is got up and gone to bring in May.
A deal of youth, ere this, is come
Back, and with white-thorn laden home.
Some have despatched their cakes and cream,
Before that we have left to dream:
And some have wept and wooed, and plighted troth,
And chose their priest, ere we can cast off sloth:
Many a green-gown has been given,
Many a kiss, both odd and even:
Many a glance, too, has been sent
From out the eye, love's firmament:
Many a jest told of the keys betraying
This night, and locks picked: yet we're not a-Maying.

Come, let us go, while we are in our prime,
And take the harmless folly of the time!
We shall grow old apace, and die
Before we know our liberty.
Our life is short, and our days run
As fast away as does the sun:—
And, as a vapour or a drop of rain,
Once lost, can ne'er be found again,
So when or you or I are made
A fable, song, or fleeting shade,
All love, all liking, all delight
Lies drowned with us in endless night.
Then, while time serves, and we are but decaying,
Come, my Corinna! come, let 's go a-Maying.

ENGLISH LYRICS

SONG

W. DRUMMOND

PHŒBUS, arise!
And paint the sable skies
With azure, white, and red;
Rouse Memnon's mother from her Tithon's bed,
That she thy career may with roses spread;
The nightingales thy coming each-where sing;
Make an eternal Spring,
Give life to this dark world which lieth dead;
Spread forth thy golden hair
In larger locks than thou wast wont before,
And emperor-like decore
With diadem of pearl thy temples fair:
Chase hence the ugly night
Which serves but to make dear thy glorious light.

This is that happy morn
That day, long wishèd day
Of all my life so dark
(If cruel stars have not my ruin sworn
And fates not hope betray),
Which, only white, deserves
A diamond for ever should it mark:
This is the morn should bring unto this grove
My Love, to hear and recompense my love.
Fair King, who all preserves,
But show thy blushing beams,
And thou two sweeter eyes
Shalt see, than those which by Penéus' streams
Did once thy heart surprise:
Nay, suns, which shine as clear
As thou when two thou did to Rome appear.
Now, Flora, deck thyself in fairest guise:
If that ye winds would hear

AND THOU TWO SWEETER EYES
SHALT SEE, THAN THOSE WHICH BY PENÉUS' STREAMS
DID ONCE THY HEART SURPRISE

SPENSER TO MILTON

A voice surpassing far Amphion's lyre,
Your stormy chiding stay;
Let zephyr only breathe
And with her tresses play,
Kissing sometimes those purple ports of death.

The winds all silent are;
And Phœbus in his chair
Ensaffroning sea and air
Makes vanish every star:
Night like a drunkard reels
Beyond the hills to shun his flaming wheels:
The fields with flowers are decked in every hue,
The clouds bespangle with bright gold their blue:
Here is the pleasant place,
And everything, save her, who all should grace.

MADRIGAL

ANON.

SISTER, awake! close not your eyes!
The day her light discloses,
And the bright morning doth arise
Out of her bed of roses.

See, the clear sun, the world's bright eye,
In at our window peeping:
Lo! how he blusheth to espy
Us idle wenches sleeping.

Therefore, awake! make haste, I say,
And let us, without staying,
All in our gowns of green so gay
Into the park a-maying.

SPRING

T. NASH

SPRING, the sweet Spring, is the year's pleasant king;
Then blooms each thing, then maids dance in a ring,
Cold doth not sting, the pretty birds do sing—
  Cuckoo, jug-jug, pu-we, to-witta-woo!

The palm and may, make country houses gay,
Lambs frisk and play, the shepherds pipe all day,
And we hear aye birds tune this merry lay—
  Cuckoo, jug-jug, pu-we, to-witta-woo!

The fields breathe sweet, the daisies kiss our feet,
Young lovers meet, old wives a-sunning sit,
In every street these tunes our ears do greet—
  Cuckoo, jug-jug, pu-we, to-witta-woo!
    Spring, the sweet Spring!

PHILLIDA AND CORYDON

N. BRETON

IN the merry month of May,
On a morn by break of day,
Forth I walked by the wood-side
Whenas May was in his pride:
There I spyed all alone
Phillida and Corydon.
Much ado there was, God wot!
He would love and she would not.
She said, never man was true;
He said, none was false to you.
She said, Love should have no wrong;
He said, he had loved her long.
Corydon would kiss her then;
She said, maids must kiss no men

PHILLIDA AND CORYDON

Till they did for good and all;
Then she made the shepherd call
All the heavens to witness truth
Never loved a truer youth.
Thus with many a pretty oath,
Yea and nay, and faith and troth,
Such as silly shepherds use
When they will not Love abuse,
Love, which long had been deluded,
Was with kisses sweet concluded;
And Phillida, with garlands gay,
Was made the Lady of the May.

THE PASSIONATE SHEPHERD TO HIS LOVE

C. MARLOWE

COME live with me and be my Love,
And we will all the pleasures prove
That hills and valleys, dales and fields,
Or woods or steepy mountain yields.

And we will sit upon the rocks,
And see the shepherds feed their flocks
By shallow rivers to whose falls
Melodious birds sing madrigals.

And I will make thee beds of roses
And a thousand fragrant posies;
A cap of flowers, and a kirtle
Embroidered all with leaves of myrtle.

A gown made of the finest wool
Which from our pretty lambs we pull;
Fair-linèd slippers for the cold,
With buckles of the purest gold.

A belt of straw and ivy-buds
With coral clasps and amber studs:
And if these pleasures may thee move,
Come live with me and be my Love.

Thy silver dishes for thy meat
As precious as the gods do eat,
Shall on an ivory table be
Prepared each day for thee and me.

The shepherd swains shall dance and sing
For thy delight each May morning:
If these delights thy mind may move,
Then live with me and be my Love.

HER REPLY

SIR W. RALEIGH (?)

If all the world and love were young,
And truth in every shepherd's tongue,
These pretty pleasures might me move
To live with thee and be thy Love.

But Time drives flocks from field to fold,
Where rivers rage and rocks grow cold;
And Philomel becometh dumb;
The rest complains of cares to come.

The flowers do fade, the wanton fields
To wayward winter reckoning yields:
A honey tongue, a heart of gall,
Is fancy's spring but sorrow's fall.

IF ALL THE WORLD AND LOVE WERE YOUNG

SPENSER TO MILTON

Thy gowns, thy shoes, thy beds of roses,
Thy cap, thy kirtle, and thy posies,
Soon break, soon wither—soon forgotten,
In folly ripe, in reason rotten.

Thy belt of straw and ivy-buds,
Thy coral clasps and amber studs,—
All these in me no means can move
To come to thee and be thy Love.

But could youth last, and love still breed,
Had joys no date, nor age no need,
Then those delights my mind might move
To live with thee and be thy Love.

IT WAS A LOVER AND HIS LASS

W. SHAKESPEARE

It was a lover and his lass,
  With a hey, and a ho, and a hey nonino,
That o'er the green corn-field did pass,
  In spring time, the only pretty ring time,
When birds do sing, hey ding a ding, ding;
Sweet lovers love the spring.

And, therefore, take the present time
  With a hey, and a ho, and a hey nonino,
For love is crownèd with the prime
  In spring time, the only pretty ring time,
When birds do sing, hey ding a ding, ding;
Sweet lovers love the spring.

Between the acres of the rye,
  With a hey, and a ho, and a hey nonino,
These pretty country folks would lie,

In spring time, the only pretty ring time,
When birds do sing, hey ding a ding, ding;
Sweet lovers love the spring.

This carol they began that hour,
With a hey, and a ho, and a hey nonino,
How that a life was but a flower
In spring time, the only pretty ring time,
When birds do sing, hey ding a ding, ding;
Sweet lovers love the spring.

WHEN DAFFODILS BEGIN TO PEER

W. SHAKESPEARE

WHEN daffodils begin to peer,
With heigh! the doxy over the dale,
Why, then comes in the sweet o' the year;
For the red blood reigns in the winter's pale.

The white sheet bleaching on the hedge,
With heigh! the sweet birds, O, how they sing!
Doth set my pugging[1] tooth on edge;
For a quart of ale is a dish for a king.

The lark that tirra-lirra chants,
With heigh! with heigh! the thrush and the jay,
Are summer songs for me and my aunts,
While we lie tumbling in the hay.

[1] Thievish.

SPENSER TO MILTON

TO DAFFODILS

R. HERRICK

FAIR daffodils, we weep to see
  You haste away so soon;
As yet the early-rising sun
  Has not attained his noon.
      Stay, stay
    Until the hasting day
          Has run
    But to the evensong;
And, having prayed together, we
Will go with you along.

We have short time to stay, as you,
  We have as short a Spring;
As quick a growth to meet decay,
  As you, or anything.
      We die
    As your hours do, and dry
          Away,
    Like to the summer's rain;
Or as the pearls of morning's dew,
Ne'er to be found again.

WHEN DAISIES PIED

W. SHAKESPEARE

WHEN daisies pied and violets blue,
  And lady-smocks all silver-white,
And cuckoo-buds of yellow hue
  Do paint the meadows with delight,
The cuckoo then, on every tree,
Mocks married men; for thus sings he
      Cuckoo;
Cuckoo, cuckoo: O word of fear,
Unpleasing to a married ear!

When shepherds pipe on oaten straws,
  And merry larks are ploughmen's clocks,
When turtles tread, and rooks, and daws,
  And maidens bleach their summer smocks,
The cuckoo then, on every tree,
  Mocks married men; for thus sings he,
          Cuckoo;
Cuckoo, cuckoo: O word of fear,
Unpleasing to the married ear!

When icicles hang by the wall,
  And Dick the shepherd blows his nail,
And Tom bears logs into the hall,
  And milk comes frozen home in pail,
When blood is nipt, and ways be foul,
Then nightly sings the staring owl,
          To-whit;
To-who, a merry note,
While greasy Joan doth keel the pot.

When all around the wind doth blow,
  And coughing drowns the parson's saw,
And birds sit brooding in the snow,
  And Marian's nose looks red and raw,
When roasted crabs hiss in the bowl,
Then nightly sings the staring owl,
          To-whit;
To-who a merry note,
While greasy Joan doth keel the pot.

SPENSER TO MILTON

ON A DAY—ALACK THE DAY

W. SHAKESPEARE

ON a day—alack the day!—
Love, whose month is ever May,
Spied a blossom passing fair
Playing in the wanton air:
Through the velvet leaves the wind,
All unseen, 'gan passage find;
That the Lover, sick to death,
Wished himself the heaven's breath.
"Air," quoth he, "thy cheeks may blow;
Air, would I might triumph so!
But, alack, my hand is sworn
Ne'er to pluck thee from thy thorn:
Vow, alack, for youth unmeet;
Youth so apt to pluck a sweet.
Do not call it sin in me,
That I am forsworn for thee;
Thou for whom Jove would swear
Juno but an Ethiope were;
And deny himself for Jove,
Turning mortal for thy love.

SONG ON MAY MORNING

J. MILTON

NOW the bright morning-star, day's harbinger,
Comes dancing from the east, and leads with her
The flowery May, who from her green lap throws
The yellow cowslip, and the pale primrose.
Hail, bounteous May, that dost inspire
Mirth and youth and warm desire!
Woods and groves are of thy dressing,
  Hill and dale doth boast thy blessing.
Thus we salute thee with our early song,
  And welcome thee, and wish thee long.

SILVIA

W. SHAKESPEARE

WHO is Silvia? What is she,
  That all our swains commend her?
Holy, fair and wise is she;
  The heaven such grace did lend her,
That she might admired be.

Is she kind as she is fair?
  For beauty lives with kindness:
Love doth to her eyes repair,
  To help him of his blindness;
And, being helped, inhabits there.

Then to Silvia let us sing,
  That Silvia is excelling;
She excels each mortal thing
  Upon the dull earth dwelling:
To her let us garlands bring.

WHO IS SILVIA? WHAT IS SHE
THAT ALL OUR SWAINS COMMEND HER?

SPENSER TO MILTON

TO THE VIRGINS, TO MAKE MUCH OF TIME

R. HERRICK

GATHER ye rosebuds while ye may,
  Old Time is still a-flying:
And this same flower that smiles to-day
  To-morrow will be dying.

The glorious lamp of heaven, the Sun,
  The higher he 's a-getting,
The sooner will his race be run,
  And nearer he 's to setting.

That age is best which is the first,
  When youth and blood are warmer;
But being spent, the worse, and worst
  Times, still succeed the former.

Then be not coy, but use your time,
  And while ye may, go marry:
For having lost but once your prime
  You may for ever tarry.

ENGLISH LYRICS

YOU SAY YOU LOVE ME

ANON.

You say you love me, nay, can swear it too;
But stay, sir, 'twill not do.
I know you keep your oaths
Just as you wear your clothes,
While new and fresh in fashion;
  But once grown old
  You lay them by,
Forgot like words you speak in passion.
I'll not believe you, I.

O MISTRESS MINE

W. SHAKESPEARE

O MISTRESS mine, where are you roaming?
O, stay and hear; your true love 's coming
  That can sing both high and low:
Trip no further, pretty sweeting;
Journeys end in lovers' meeting,
  Every wise man's son doth know.

What is Love? 'tis not hereafter;
Present mirth hath present laughter;
  What 's to come is still unsure:
In delay there lies no plenty;
Then come kiss me, Sweet-and-twenty,
  Youth 's a stuff will not endure.

THEN COME KISS ME, SWEET-AND-TWENTY
YOUTH 'S A STUFF WILL NOT ENDURE

SPENSER TO MILTON

A MAID'S SONG

T. CAMPION

" MAIDS are simple," some men say,
"They forsooth will trust no men;"
But should they men's wills obey,
Maids were very simple then.

Truth a rare flower now is grown,
Few men wear it in their hearts;
Lovers are more easily known
By their follies than deserts.

Safer may we credit give
To a faithless, wandering Jew,
Than a young man's vows believe
When he swears his love is true.

Love they make a poor blind child,
But let none trust such as he;
Rather than to be beguiled,
Ever let me simple be.

LOVE IN THY YOUTH

ANON.

LOVE in thy youth, fair Maid, be wise;
Old Time will make thee colder,
And though each morning new arise,
Yet we each day grow older.
Thou as Heaven art fair and young,
Thine eyes like twin stars shining;
But ere another day be sprung
All these will be declining.
Then winter comes with all his fears,
And all thy sweets shall borrow;
Too late then wilt thou shower thy tears,—
And I too late shall sorrow!

SONG

E. WALLER

Go, lovely Rose!
Tell her, that wastes her time and me,
That now she knows,
When I resemble her to thee,
How sweet and fair she seems to be.

Tell her that's young
And shuns to have her graces spied,
That hadst thou sprung
In deserts, where no men abide,
Thou must have uncommended died.

Small is the worth
Of beauty from the light retired:
Bid her come forth,
Suffer herself to be desired,
And not blush so to be admired.

Then die! that she
The common fate of all things rare
May read in thee:
How small a part of time they share
That are so wondrous sweet and fair!

A COUNSEL FOR MAIDS

T. CAMPION

Never love unless you can
Bear with all the faults of man;
Men sometimes will jealous be,
Though but little cause they see,
And hang the head as discontent,
And speak what straight they will repent.

SPENSER TO MILTON

Men that but one saint adore,
Make a show of love to more;
Beauty must be scorned in none,
Though but truly served in one:
For what is courtship but disguise?
True hearts may have dissembling eyes.

Men, when their affairs require,
Must awhile themselves retire;
Sometimes hunt and sometimes hawk,
And not ever sit and talk:
If these and such-like you can bear,
Then like and love, and never fear!

IF WOMEN COULD BE FAIR AND NEVER FOND

E. VERE, EARL OF OXFORD

If women could be fair and never fond,
Or that their beauty might continue still,
I would not marvel though they made men bond
By service long to purchase their goodwill:
But when I see how frail these creatures are,
I laugh that men forget themselves so far.

To mark what choice they make and how they change,
How, leaving best, the worst they choose out still;
And how, like haggards wild, about they range,
And scorning reason follow after will!
Who would not shake such buzzards from the fist
And let them fly (fair fools!) which way they list?

Yet for our sport we fawn and flatter both,
To pass the time when nothing else can please:
And train them on to yield by subtle oath
The sweet content that gives such humour ease:
And then we say, when we their follies try,
"To play with fools, O, what a fool was I!"

PHILOMELA

SIR P. SIDNEY

THE Nightingale, as soon as April bringeth
Unto her rested sense a perfect waking,
While late-bare Earth, proud of new clothing, springeth,
Sings out her woes, a thorn her song-book making;
And mournfully bewailing,
Her throat in tunes expresseth
What grief her breast oppresseth,
For Tereus' force on her chaste will prevailing.
O Philomela fair, O take some gladness
That here is juster cause of plaintful sadness!
Thine earth now springs, mine fadeth;
Thy thorn without, my thorn my heart invadeth.

Alas! she hath no other cause of anguish
But Tereus' love, on her by strong hand wroken;
Wherein she suffering, all her spirits languish,
Full womanlike complains her will was broken.
But I, who, daily craving,
Cannot have to content me,
Have more cause to lament me,
Since wanting is more woe than too much having.
O Philomela fair, O take some gladness
That here is juster cause of plaintful sadness!
Thine earth now springs, mine fadeth;
Thy thorn without, my thorn my heart invadeth.

SPENSER TO MILTON

THE SEA HATH MANY THOUSAND SANDS

ANON

THE sea hath many thousand sands,
The sun hath motes as many;
The sky is full of stars, and Love
As full of woes as any:
Believe me, that do know the elf,
And make no trial by thyself.

It is in truth a pretty toy
For babes to play withal;
But O, the honeys of our youth
Are oft our age's gall!
Self-proof in time will make thee know
He was a prophet told thee so:

A prophet that, Cassandra-like,
Tells truth without belief;
For headstrong Youth will run his race,
Although his goal be grief:
Love's Martyr, when his heat is past,
Proves Care's Confessor at the last.

OVER THE MOUNTAINS

ANON

OVER the mountains
And over the waves,
Under the fountains
And under the graves;
Under floods that are deepest,
Which Neptune obey;
Over rocks that are steepest
Love will find out the way.

Where there is no place
For the glow-worm to lie ;
Where there is no space
For receipt of a fly ;
Where the midge dares not venture
Lest herself fast she lay ;
If Love come, he will enter
And soon find out his way.

You may esteem him
A child for his might ;
Or you may deem him
A coward from his flight ;
But if she whom love doth honour
Be concealed from the day,
Set a thousand guards upon her,
Love will find out the way.

Some think to lose him
By having him confined ;
And some do suppose him,
Poor thing, to be blind ;
But if ne'er so close you wall him,
Do the best that you may,
Blind Love, if so ye call him,
Will find out his way.

You may train the eagle
To stoop to your fist ;
Or you may inveigle
The phœnix of the east :
The lioness, ye may move her
To give o'er her prey ;
But you'll ne'er stop a lover :
He will find out his way.

SPENSER TO MILTON

LOVE ME OR NOT, LOVE HER I MUST OR DIE

T. CAMPION

LOVE me or not, love her I must or die ;
Leave me or not, follow her needs must I.
O that her grace would my wished comforts give !
How rich in her, how happy I should live !

All my desire, all my delight should be
Her to enjoy, her to unite to me ;
Envy should cease, her would I love alone :
Who loves by looks is seldom true to one.

Could I enchant, and that it lawful were,
Her would I charm softly that none should hear ;
But love enforced rarely yields firm content :
So would I love that neither should repent.

TAKE, O TAKE THOSE LIPS AWAY

W. SHAKESPEARE

TAKE, O take those lips away,
  That so sweetly were forsworn;
And those eyes, the break of day,
  Lights that do mislead the morn:
But my kisses bring again,
        Bring again;
Seals of love, but sealed in vain,
        Sealed in vain!

UNDER THE GREENWOOD TREE

W. SHAKESPEARE

UNDER the greenwood tree,
Who loves to lie with me,
And tune his merry note
Unto the sweet bird's throat,
Come hither, come hither, come hither:
Here shall he see
No enemy
But winter and rough weather.

Who doth ambition shun,
And loves to live i' the sun,
Seeking the food he eats,
And pleased with what he gets,
Come hither, come hither, come hither;
Here shall he see
No enemy
But winter and rough weather.

COME, you pretty false-eyed wanton,
  Leave your crafty smiling!
Think you to escape me now
  With slipp'ry words beguiling?
No; you mocked me t' other day;
When you got loose, you fled away;
But, since I have caught you now,
  I'll clip your wings for flying:
Smoth'ring kisses fast I'll heap,
  And keep you so from crying.

Sooner may you count the stars
  And number hail down-pouring,
Tell the osiers of the Thames,
  Or Goodwin sands devouring,
Than the thick-showered kisses here
Which now thy tired lips must bear.
Such a harvest never was
  So rich and full of pleasure,
But 'tis spent as soon as reaped,
  So trustless is Love's treasure.

SPENSER TO MILTON

SONNET

SIR P. SIDNEY

O KISS, which dost those ruddy gems impart,
Or gems or fruits of new-found Paradise,
Breathing all bliss and sweetness to the heart,
Teaching dumb lips a nobler exercise;
O kiss, which souls, even souls, together ties
By links of love and only Nature's art,
How fain would I paint thee to all men's eyes,
Or of thy gifts at least shade out some part!
But she forbids; with blushing words she says
She builds her fame on higher-seated praise.
But my heart burns; I cannot silent be.
Then since, dear Life, you fain would have me peace,
And I, mad with delight, want wit to cease,
Stop you my mouth with still, still kissing me.

TO ELECTRA

R. HERRICK

I DARE not ask a kiss,
  I dare not beg a smile,
Lest having that or this
  I might grow proud the while.

No! no! the utmost share
  Of my desire shall be,
Only to kiss that air
  That lately kissèd thee.

CLAIMING A KISS

B. JONSON

FOR Love's sake, kiss me once again,
I long, and should not beg in vain,
Here 's none to spy, or see,
Why do you doubt or stay?
I'll taste as lightly as the bee,
That doth but touch his flower, and flies away.

Once more, and, faith, I will be gone;
Can he that loves ask less than one?
Nay, you may err in this,
And all your bounty wrong;
This could be called but half a kiss:
What we're but once to do, we should do long.

MY TRUE LOVE HATH MY HEART

SIR P. SIDNEY

MY true love hath my heart, and I have his,
By just exchange one for the other given:
I hold his dear, and mine he cannot miss,
There never was a better bargain driven:
His heart in me keeps me and him in one,
My heart in him his thoughts and senses guides:
He loves my heart, for once it was his own,
I cherish his because in me it bides:
My true love hath my heart, and I have his.

SPENSER TO MILTON

FAIN WOULD I CHANGE THAT NOTE

ANON.

FAIN would I change that note
To which fond Love hath charmed me
Long long to sing by rote,
Fancying that that harmed me:
Yet when this thought doth come,
" Love is the perfect sum
    Of all delight,"
I have no other choice
Either for pen or voice
    To sing or write.

O Love! they wrong thee much
That say thy sweet is bitter,
When thy rich fruit is such
As nothing can be sweeter.
Fair house of joy and bliss,
Where truest pleasure is,
    I do adore thee:
I know thee what thou art,
I serve thee with my heart,
    And fall before thee!

LOVE GUARDS THE ROSES OF THY LIPS

T. LODGE

LOVE guards the roses of thy lips
  And flies about them like a bee;
If I approach he forward skips,
  And if I kiss he stingeth me.

Love in thine eyes doth build his bower,
  And sleeps within his pretty shrine;
And if I look the boy will lower,
  And from their orbs shoot shafts divine.

Love works thy heart within his fire,
  And in my tears doth firm the same;
And if I tempt it will retire,
  And of my plaints doth make a game.

Love, let me cull her choicest flowers;
  And pity me, and calm her eye;
Make soft her heart, dissolve her lowers;
  Then will I praise thy deity.

But if thou do not, Love, I'll truly serve her
In spite of thee, and by firm faith deserve her.

SONNET

W. SHAKESPEARE

SHALL I compare thee to a summer's day?
Thou art more lovely and more temperate:
Rough winds do shake the darling buds of May,
And summer's lease hath all too short a date:
Sometime too hot the eye of heaven shines,
And often is his gold complexion dimmed;
And every fair from fair sometime declines,
By chance or nature's changing course untrimmed.
But thy eternal summer shall not fade
Nor lose possession of that fair thou owest;
Nor shall Death brag thou wanderest in his shade,
When in eternal lines to time thou growest:
So long as men can breathe, or eyes can see,
So long lives this,—and this gives life to thee.

SPENSER TO MILTON

SONNET

SIR P. SIDNEY

HIGH-WAY, since you my chief Parnassus be,
And that my Muse, to some ears not unsweet,
Tempers her words to trampling horses' feet
More oft than to a chamber-melody,—
Now, blessèd you bear onward blessèd me
To her, where I my heart, safe-left, shall meet;
My Muse and I must you of duty greet
With thanks and wishes, wishing thankfully;
Be you still fair, honoured by public heed;
By no encroachment wronged, nor time forgot;
Nor blamed for blood, nor shamed for sinful deed;
And that you know I envy you no lot
Of highest wish, I wish you so much bliss,—
Hundreds of years you Stella's feet may kiss!

SONG

T. CAREW

ASK me no more where Jove bestows,
When June is past, the fading rose;
For in your beauty's orient deep
These flowers, as in their causes, sleep.

Ask me no more whither do stray
The golden atoms of the day;
For in pure love heaven did prepare
Those powders to enrich your hair.

Ask me no more whither doth haste
The nightingale when May is past;
For in your sweet dividing throat
She winters and keeps warm her note.

Ask me no more where those stars light
That downwards fall in dead of night;
For in your eyes they sit, and there
Fixèd become as in their sphere.

Ask me no more if east or west
The Phœnix builds her spicy nest;
For unto you at last she flies,
And in your fragrant bosom dies.

SIGH NO MORE, LADIES

W. SHAKESPEARE

SIGH no more, ladies, sigh no more;
  Men were deceivers ever;
One foot in sea, and one on shore,
  To one thing constant never.
      Then sigh not so,
      But let them go,
    And be you blithe and bonny,
Converting all your sounds of woe
  Into Hey nonny, nonny.

Sing no more ditties, sing no moe,
  Of dumps so dull and heavy;
The fraud of men was ever so,
  Since summer first was leafy.
      Then sigh not so,
      But let them go,
    And be you blithe and bonny,
Converting all your sounds of woe
  Into Hey nonny, nonny.

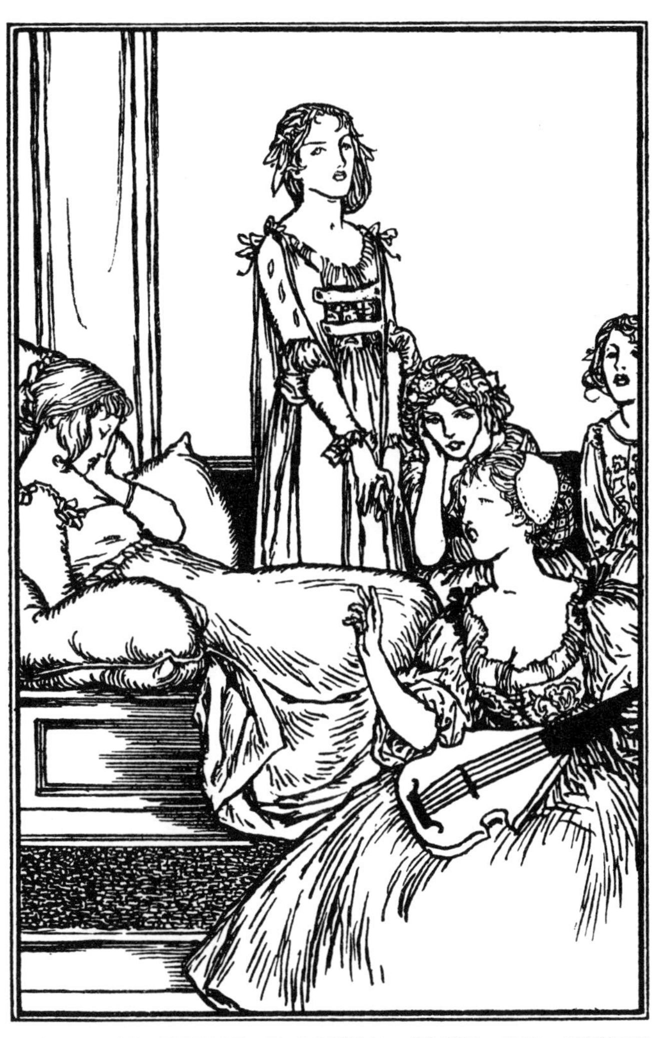

SIGH NO MORE, LADIES, SIGH NO MORE
MEN WERE DECEIVERS EVER

SPENSER TO MILTON

ROSALINE

T. LODGE

LIKE to the clear in highest sphere
  Where all imperial glory shines,
Of selfsame colour is her hair
  Whether unfolded or in twines :
      Heigh ho, fair Rosaline!
Her eyes are sapphires set in snow,
  Resembling heaven by every wink ;
The gods do fear whenas they glow,
  And I do tremble when I think
      Heigh ho, would she were mine!

Her cheeks are like the blushing cloud
  That beautifies Aurora's face,
Or like the silver crimson shroud
  That Phœbus' smiling looks doth grace:
      Heigh ho, fair Rosaline!
Her lips are like two budded roses
  Whom ranks of lilies neighbour nigh,
Within whose bounds she balm encloses
  Apt to entice a deity :
      Heigh ho, would she were mine!

Her neck is like a stately tower
  Where Love himself imprisoned lies,
To watch for glances every hour
  From her divine and sacred eyes :
      Heigh ho, fair Rosaline!
Her paps are centres of delight,
  Her breasts are orbs of heavenly frame,
Where Nature moulds the dew of light
  To feed perfection with the same :
      Heigh ho, would she were mine!

With orient pearl, with ruby red,
  With marble white, with sapphire blue,
Her body every way is fed,

Yet soft in touch and sweet in view:
Heigh ho, fair Rosaline!
Nature herself her shape admires;
The gods are wounded in her sight;
And Love forsakes his heavenly fires
And at her eyes his brand doth light:
Heigh ho, would she were mine!

Then muse not, Nymphs, though I bemoan
The absence of fair Rosaline,
Since for a fair there 's fairer none,
Nor for her virtues so divine:
Heigh ho, fair Rosaline!
Heigh ho, my heart! would God that she were mine!

CUPID AND CAMPASPÉ

J. LYLY

CUPID and my Campaspé played
At cards for kisses—Cupid paid:
He stakes his quiver, bow, and arrows,
His mother's doves, and team of sparrows;
Loses them too; then down he throws
The coral of his lip, the rose
Growing on 's cheek (but none knows how);
With these, the crystal of his brow,
And then the dimple of his chin:
All these did my Campaspé win.
At last he set her both his eyes—
She won, and Cupid blind did rise.
O Love! has she done this to thee?
What shall, alas! become of me?

CUPID AND MY CAMPASPÉ PLAYED
AT CARDS FOR KISSES

EPITHALAMION

EDMUND SPENSER

YE LEARNED SISTERS, WHICH HAVE OFTENTIMES
BEEN TO THE AIDING OTHERS TO ADORN

SPENSER TO MILTON

EPITHALAMION

E. SPENSER

YE learned sisters, which have oftentimes
Been to the aiding others to adorn,
Whom ye thought worthy of your graceful rhymes,
That even the greatest did not greatly scorn
To hear their names sung in your simple lays,
But joyèd in their praise;
And when ye list your own mishaps to mourn,
Which death, or love, or fortune's wreck did raise,
Your string could soon to sadder tenor turn,
And teach the woods and waters to lament
Your doleful dreariment:
Now lay those sorrowful complaints aside;
And having all your heads with garland crowned,
Help me mine own Love's praises to resound;
Nor let the same of any be envied:
So Orpheus did for his own bride,
So I unto myself alone will sing;
The woods shall to me answer, and my echo ring.

Early, before the world's light-giving lamp
His golden beam upon the hills doth spread,
Having dispersed the night's uncheerful damp,
Do ye awake; and with fresh lustihead
Go to the bower of my beloved Love,
My truest turtle dove:
Bid her awake; for Hymen is awake,
And long since ready forth his mask to move,
With his bright tead[1] that flames with many a flake,
And many a bachelor to wait on him,
In their fresh garments trim.
Bid her awake therefore, and soon her dight,
For lo! the wishèd day is come at last,

[1] Torch.

That shall for all the pains and sorrows past
Pay to her usury of long delight :
And, whilst she doth her dight,
Do ye to her of joy and solace sing,
That all the woods may answer, and your echo ring.

Bring with you all the nymphs that you can hear
Both of the rivers and the forests green,
And of the sea that neighbours to her near ;
All with gay garlands goodly well beseen.
And let them also with them bring in hand
Another gay garland,
For my fair Love, of lilies and of roses,
Bound truelove wise, with a blue silk riband.
And let them make great store of bridal posies,
And let them eke bring store of other flowers,
To deck the bridal bowers.
And let the ground whereas her foot shall tread,
For fear the stones her tender foot should wrong,
Be strewed with fragrant flowers all along,
And diapered like the discoloured mead.
Which done, do at her chamber door await,
For she will waken straight,
The while do ye this song unto her sing ;
The woods shall to you answer, and your echo ring.

Ye nymphs of Mulla, which with careful heed
The silver scaly trouts do tend full well,
And greedy pikes which use therein to feed ;
(Those trouts and pikes all others do excel ;)
And ye likewise, which keep the rushy lake
Where none do fishes take,
Bind up the locks the which hang scattered light,
And in his waters, which your mirror make,
Behold your faces as the crystal bright,
That when you come whereas my Love doth lie,
No blemish she may spy.

And eke, ye lightfoot maids, which keep the door,
That on the hoary mountain use to tower,
And the wild wolves which seek them to devour,
With your steel darts do chase from coming near ;
Be also present here,
To help to deck her, and to help to sing,
That all the woods may answer, and your echo ring.

Wake now, my Love, awake! for it is time ;
The rosy Morn long since left Tithon's bed,
All ready to her silver coach to climb ;
And Phœbus 'gins to show his glorious head.
Hark ! how the cheerful birds do chant their lays,
And carol of love's praise.
The merry lark her matins sings aloft ;
The thrush replies ; the mavis descant plays ;
The ousel shrills ; the ruddock warbles soft ;
So goodly all agree with sweet consent
To this day's merriment.
Ah ! my dear Love, why do ye sleep thus long,
When meeter were that ye should now awake,
T' await the coming of your joyous make,[1]
And hearken to the birds' lovelearned song,
The dewy leaves among ?
For they of joy and pleasance to you sing,
That all the woods them answer, and their echo ring.

My Love is now awake out of her dreams,
And her fair eyes, like stars that dimmèd were
With darksome cloud, now show their goodly beams
More bright than Hesperus his head doth rear.
Come now, ye damsels, daughters of delight,
Help quickly her to dight :
But first come, ye fair hours, which were begot,
In Jove's sweet paradise, of Day and Night ;
Which do the seasons of the year allot,

[1] Mate.

And all that ever in this world is fair
Do make and still repair:
And ye three handmaids of the Cyprian Queen,
The which do still adorn her beauty's pride,
Help to adorn my beautifulest bride:
And, as ye her array, still throw between
Some graces to be seen;
And, as ye use to Venus, to her sing,
The while the woods shall answer, and your echo ring.

Now is my Love all ready forth to come:
Let all the virgins therefore well await;
And ye, fresh boys, that tend upon her groom,
Prepare yourselves, for he is coming straight.
Set all your things in seemly good array,
Fit for so joyful day:
The joyful'st day that ever sun did see.
Fair Sun! show forth thy favourable ray,
And let thy lifefull heat not fervent be,
For fear of burning her sunshiny face,
Her beauty to disgrace.
O fairest Phœbus! father of the Muse!
If ever I did honour thee aright,
Or sing the thing that might thy mind delight,
Do not thy servant's simple boon refuse;
But let this day, let this one day, be mine;
Let all the rest be thine:
Then I thy sovereign praises loud will sing,
That all the woods shall answer, and their echo ring.

Hark! how the minstrels 'gin to shrill aloud
Their merry music that resounds from far,
The pipe, the tabor, and the trembling crowd,
That well agree withouten breach or jar.
But most of all the damsels do delight,
When they their timbrels smite,
And thereunto do dance and carol sweet,

That all the senses they do ravish quite;
The while the boys run up and down the street,
Crying aloud with strong confusèd noise,
As if it were one voice,
Hymen! ïo Hymen! Hymen! they do shout;
That even to the heavens their shouting shrill
Doth reach, and all the firmament doth fill:
To which the people standing all about,
As in approvance, do thereto applaud,
And loud advance her laud;
And evermore they Hymen, Hymen, sing,
That all the woods them answer, and their echo ring.

Lo! where she comes along with portly pace,
Like Phœbe from her chamber of the East,
Arising forth to run her mighty race,
Clad all in white, that 'seems a virgin best.
So well it her beseems, that ye would ween
Some angel she had been.
Her long loose yellow locks like golden wire,
Sprinkled with pearl, and pearling flowers atween,
Do like a golden mantle her attire;
And being crownèd with a garland green,
Seem like some maiden Queen.
Her modest eyes, abashèd to behold
So many gazers as on her do stare,
Upon the lowly ground affixèd are;
Nor dare lift up her countenance too bold,
But blush to hear her praises sung so loud,
So far from being proud.
Nathless, do ye still loud her praises sing,
That all the woods may answer, and your echo ring.

Tell me, ye merchants' daughters, did ye see
So fair a creature in your town before,
So sweet, so lovely, and so mild as she,
Adorned with beauty's grace and virtue's store?

Her goodly eyes like sapphires shining bright,
Her forehead ivory white,
Her cheeks like apples which the sun hath rudded,
Her lips like cherries charming men to bite,
Her breast like to a bowl of cream uncrudded,
Her paps like lilies budded,
Her snowy neck like to a marble tower ;
And all her body like a palace fair,
Ascending up, with many a stately stair,
To honour's seat and chastity's sweet bower.
Why stand ye still, ye virgins, in amaze
Upon her so to gaze,
While ye forget your former lay to sing,
To which the woods did answer, and your echo ring?

But if ye saw that which no eyes can see,
The inward beauty of her lively spright,
Garnished with heavenly gifts of high degree,
Much more then would ye wonder at that sight,
And stand astonished like to those which read
Medusa's mazeful head.
There dwells sweet love, and constant chastity,
Unspotted faith, and comely womanhood,
Regard of honour, and mild modesty ;
There virtue reigns as queen in royal throne,
And giveth laws alone,
The which the base affections do obey,
And yield their services unto her will ;
Nor thought of things uncomely ever may
Thereto approach to tempt her mind to ill.
Had ye once seen these her celestial treasures,
And unrevealed pleasures,
Then would ye wonder, and her praises sing,
That all the woods should answer, and your echo ring.

Open the temple gates unto my Love!
Open them wide that she may enter in,

And all the posts adorn as doth behove
And all the pillars deck with garlands trim,
For to receive this Saint with honour due
That cometh in to you.
With trembling steps, and humble reverence,
She cometh in before th' Almighty's view.
Of her, ye virgins, learn obedience,
When so ye come into those holy places,
To humble your proud faces.
Bring her up to th' high altar, that she may
The sacred ceremonies there partake,
The which do endless matrimony make;
And let the roaring organs loudly play
The praises of the Lord in lively notes;
The while, with hollow throats,
The choristers the joyous anthem sing,
That all the woods may answer, and their echo ring.

Behold, while she before the altar stands,
Hearing the holy priest that to her speaks,
And blesseth her with his two happy hands,
How the red roses flush up in her cheeks,
And the pure snow, with goodly vermeil stain,
Like crimson dyed in grain;
That even the angels, which continually
About the sacred altar do remain,
Forget their service and about her fly,
Oft peeping in her face, that seems more fair,
The more they on it stare.
But her sad eyes, still fastened on the ground,
Are governèd with goodly modesty,
That suffers not one look to glance awry,
Which may let in a little thought unsound.
Why blush ye, Love, to give to me your hand,
The pledge of all our band?
Sing, ye sweet angels, Alleluia sing,
That all the woods may answer, and your echo ring.

Now all is done: bring home the Bride again;
Bring home the triumph of our victory;
Bring home with you the glory of her gain,
With joyance bring her and with jollity.
Never had man more joyful day than this,
Whom heaven would heap with bliss.
Make feast therefore now all this livelong day;
This day for ever to me holy is.
Pour out the wine without restraint or stay,
Pour not by cups, but by the bellyful,
Pour out to all that wull,
And sprinkle all the posts and walls with wine,
That they may sweat, and drunken be withal.
Crown ye god Bacchus with a coronal,
And Hymen also crown with wreaths of vine;
And let the Graces dance unto the rest,
For they can do it best:
The while the maidens do their carol sing,
To which the woods shall answer, and their echo ring.

Ring ye the bells, ye young men of the town,
And leave your wonted labours for this day:
This day is holy; do ye write it down,
That ye for ever it remember may.
This day the sun is in his chiefest height,
With Barnaby the bright,
From whence declining daily by degrees,
He somewhat loseth of his heat and light,
When once the Crab behind his back he sees.
But for this time it ill ordainèd was,
To choose the longest day in all the year,
And shortest night, when longest fitter were:
Yet never day so long but late would pass.
Ring ye the bells, to make it wear away,
And bonfires make all day;
And dance about them, and about them sing,
That all the woods may answer, and your echo ring.

CROWN YE GOD BACCHUS WITH A CORONAL
AND HYMEN ALSO CROWN WITH WREATHS OF VINE

Ah! when will this long weary day have end,
And lend me leave to come unto my Love?
How slowly do the hours their numbers spend;
How slowly does sad Time his feathers move!
Haste thee, O fairest Planet! to thy home
Within the Western foam:
Thy tirèd steeds long since have need of rest.
Long though it be, at last I see it gloom,
And the bright evening star with golden crest
Appear out of the East.
Fair child of beauty! glorious lamp of love!
That all the host of heaven in ranks dost lead,
And guidest lovers through the night's sad dread,
How cheerfully thou lookest from above,
And seem'st to laugh atween thy twinkling light,
As joying in the sight
Of these glad many, which for joy do sing,
That all the woods them answer, and their echo ring.

Now cease, ye damsels, your delights forepast;
Enough is it that all the day was yours:
Now day is done, and night is nighing fast,
Now bring the Bride into the bridal bowers.
The night is come, now soon her disarray,
And in her bed her lay;
Lay her in lilies and in violets,
And silken curtains over her display,
And odoured sheets, and arras coverlets.
Behold how goodly my fair Love does lie,
In proud humility!
Like unto Maia, whenas Jove her took
In Tempe, lying on the flowery grass,
'Twixt sleep and wake, after she weary was,
With bathing in the Acidalian brook.
Now it is night, ye damsels may be gone,
And leave my Love alone;
And leave likewise your former lay to sing:

The woods no more shall answer, nor your echo ring.

Now welcome, night! thou night so long expected,
That long day's labour dost at last defray,
And all my cares, which cruel love collected,
Has summed in one, and cancellèd for aye:
Spread thy broad wing over my Love and me,
That no man may us see;
And in thy sable mantle us enwrap,
From fear of peril and foul horror free.
Let no false treason seek us to entrap,
Nor any dread disquiet once annoy
The safety of our joy;
But let the night be calm and quietsome,
Without tempestuous storms or sad affray:
Like as when Jove with fair Alcmena lay,
When he begot the great Tirynthian groom:
Or like as when he with thyself did lie,
And begot Majesty.
And let the maids and young men cease to sing;
Ne let the woods them answer, nor their echo ring.

Let no lamenting cries, nor doleful tears,
Be heard all night within, nor yet without:
Ne let false whispers, breeding hidden fears,
Break gentle sleep with misconceived doubt.
Let no deluding dreams, nor dreadful sights,
Make sudden sad affrights;
Ne let housefires, nor lightning's helpless harms,
Ne let the Puck, nor other evil sprights,
Ne let mischievous witches with their charms,
Ne let hobgoblins, names whose sense we see not,
Fray us with things that be not;
Let not the screech owl, nor the stork, be heard;
Nor the night raven, that still deadly yells;
Nor damned ghosts, called up with mighty spells;
Nor grisly vultures make us once afeared:

Ne let th' unpleasant choir of frogs still croaking
Make us to wish their choking.
Let none of these their dreary accents sing;
Ne let the woods them answer, nor their echo ring.

But let still Silence true night watches keep,
That sacred peace may in assurance reign,
And timely sleep, when it is time to sleep,
May pour his limbs forth on your pleasant plain;
The while a hundred little wingèd loves,
Like divers feathered doves,
Shall fly and flutter round about the bed,
And in the secret dark, that none reproves,
Their pretty stealths shall work, and snares shall
spread
To filch away sweet snatches of delight,
Concealed through covert night.
Ye sons of Venus, play your sports at will;
For greedy pleasure, careless of your toys,
Thinks more upon her paradise of joys,
Than what ye do, albeit good or ill.
All night therefore attend your merry play,
For it will soon be day:
Now none doth hinder you, that say or sing;
Ne will the woods now answer, nor your echo ring.

Who is the same, which at my window peeps,
Or whose is that fair face that shines so bright?
Is it not Cynthia, she that never sleeps,
But walks about high heaven all the night?
O, fairest goddess! do thou not envỳ
My Love with me to spy;
For thou likewise didst love, though now unthought,
And for a fleece of wool, which privily
The Latmian shepherd once unto thee brought,
His pleasures with thee wrought.
Therefore to us be favourable now;

And sith of women's labours thou hast charge,
And generation goodly dost enlarge,
Incline thy will t' effect our wishful vow,
And the chaste womb inform with timely seed,
That may our comfort breed:
Till which we cease our hopeful hap to sing;
Ne let the woods us answer, nor our echo ring.

And thou, great Juno, which with awful might
The laws of wedlock still dost patronize,
And the religion of the faith first plight
With sacred rites hast taught to solemnize;
And eke for comfort often callèd art
Of women in their smart;
Eternally bind thou this lovely band,
And all thy blessings unto us impart.
And thou, glad Genius, in whose gentle hand
The bridal bower and genial bed remain,
Without blemish or stain;
And the sweet pleasures of their love's delight
With secret aid dost succour and supply,
Till they bring forth the fruitful progeny;
Send us the timely fruit of this same night:
And thou, fair Hebe, and thou, Hymen free,
Grant that it may so be!
Till which we cease your further praise to sing;
Ne any woods shall answer, nor your echo ring.

And ye high heavens, the temple of the gods,
In which a thousand torches flaming bright
Do burn, that to us wretched earthly clods
In dreadful darkness lend desirèd light;
And all ye powers which in the same remain,
More than we men can feign,
Pour out your blessing on us plenteously,
And happy influence upon us rain,
That we may raise a large posterity,

Which from the earth, which they may long possess
With lasting happiness,
Up to your haughty palaces may mount:
And, for the guerdon of their glorious merit,
May heavenly tabernacles there inherit,
Of blessed saints for to increase the count.
So let us rest, sweet Love, in hope of this,
And cease till then our timely joys to sing,
The woods no more us answer, nor our echo ring.

Song! made in lieu of many ornaments,
With which my Love should duly have been decked,
Which cutting off through hasty accidents,
Ye would not stay your due time to expect,
But promised both to recompense;
Be unto her a goodly ornament,
And for short time an endless monument!

WE saw and wooed each other's eyes,
My soul contracted then with thine,
And both burnt in one sacrifice,
By which our marriage grew divine.

Let wilder youth, whose soul is sense,
Profane the temple of delight,
And purchase endless penitence
With the stol'n pleasure of one night.

Time 's ever ours, while we despise
The sensual idol of our clay,
For though the sun do set and rise,
We joy one everlasting day—

Whose light no jealous clouds obscure,
While each of us shine innocent;
The troubled stream is still impure;
With virtue flies away content.

And though opinion often err,
We'll court the modest smile of fame,
For sin's black danger circles her
Who hath infection in her name.

Thus when to one dark silent room
Death shall our loving coffins thrust,
Fame will build columns on our tomb,
And add a perfume to our dust.

SPENSER TO MILTON

A BRIDAL SONG

J. FLETCHER (?)

ROSES, their sharp spines being gone,
Not royal in their smells alone,
  But in their hue ;
Maiden pinks, of odour faint,
Daisies smell-less, yet most quaint,
  And sweet thyme true ;

Primrose, firstborn child of Ver ;
Merry springtime's harbinger,
  With her bells dim ;
Oxlips in their cradles growing,
Marigolds on deathbeds blowing,
  Larks'-heels trim.

All dear Nature's children sweet
Lie 'fore bride and bridegroom's feet,
  Blessing their sense !
Not an angel of the air,
Bird melodious or bird fair,
  Be absent hence !

The crow, the slanderous cuckoo, nor
The boding raven, nor chough hoar,
  Nor chattering pye,
May on our bridehouse perch or sing,
Or with them any discord bring,
  But from it fly !

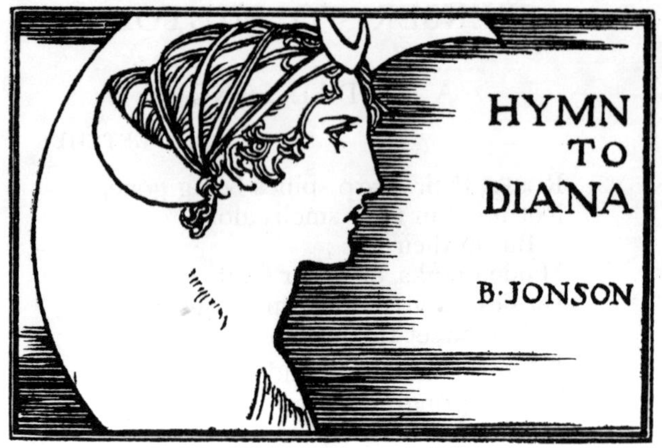

QUEEN and Huntress, chaste and fair,
  Now the sun is laid to sleep,
Seated in thy silver chair,
  State in wonted manner keep :
      Hesperus entreats thy light,
      Goddess excellently bright.

Earth, let not thy envious shade
  Dare itself to interpose ;
Cynthia's shining orb was made
  Heaven to clear when day did close :
    Bless us then with wishèd sight,
    Goddess excellently bright.

Lay thy bow of pearl apart,
  And thy crystal-shining quiver ;
Give unto the flying hart
  Space to breathe, how short soever :
      Thou that mak'st a day of night,—
      Goddess excellently bright.

TO CELIA

B. JONSON

DRINK to me only with thine eyes,
  And I will pledge with mine;
Or leave a kiss but in the cup
  And I 'll not look for wine.
The thirst that from the soul doth rise
  Doth ask a drink divine;
But might I of Jove's nectar sup,
  I would not change for thine.

I sent thee late a rosy wreath,
  Not so much honouring thee,
As giving it a hope that there
  It could not withered be;
But thou thereon didst only breathe
  And sent'st it back to me;
Since when it grows, and smells, I swear,
  Not of itself but thee!

ENGLISH LYRICS

SONG

T. CAMPION

COME, O come, my life's delight,
  Let me not in languor pine!
Love loves no delay; thy sight
  The more enjoyed, the more divine:
O come, and take from me
The pain of being deprived of thee!

Thou all sweetness dost enclose,
  Like a little world of bliss;
Beauty guards thy looks, the rose
  In them pure and eternal is:
Come, then, and make thy flight
As swift to me as heavenly light!

SONNET

W. DRUMMOND

ALEXIS, here she stayed; among these pines,
Sweet hermitress, she did alone repair;
Here did she spread the treasure of her hair,
More rich than that brought from the Colchian mines.
She sat her by these muskèd eglantines,
The happy place the print seems yet to bear;
Her voice did sweeten here thy sugared lines,
To which winds, trees, beasts, birds did lend an ear.
Me here she first perceived, and here a morn
Of bright carnations did o'erspread her face:
Here did she sigh, here first my hopes were born,
Here first I got a pledge of promised grace:
But ah! what served it to be happy so
Sith passèd pleasures double but new woe?

SPENSER TO MILTON

SONNET

W. SHAKESPEARE

So sweet a kiss the golden sun gives not
  To those fresh morning drops upon the rose,
As thy eye-beams, when their fresh rays have smote
  The night of dew that on my cheeks down flows:
Nor shines the silver moon one half so bright
  Through the transparent bosom of the deep,
As doth thy face through tears of mine give light:
  Thou shin'st in every tear that I do weep;
No drop but as a coach doth carry thee,
  So ridest thou triumphing in my woe:
Do but behold the tears that swell in me,
  And they thy glory through my grief will show:
But do not love thyself; then thou wilt keep
My tears for glasses, and still make me weep.
O Queen of queens! how far dost thou excel,
No thought can think, nor tongue of mortal tell!

THE UNFADING BEAUTY

T. CAREW

He that loves a rosy cheek,
  Or a coral lip admires,
Or from star-like eyes doth seek
  Fuel to maintain his fires:
As old Time makes these decay,
So his flames must waste away.

But a smooth and steadfast mind,
  Gentle thoughts and calm desires,
Hearts with equal love combined,
  Kindle never-dying fires:—
Where these are not, I despise
Lovely cheeks or lips or eyes.

THE DYING LOVER

SIR W. DAVENANT

DEAR Love, let me this evening die,
  Oh smile not to prevent it;
Dead with my rivals let me lie,
  Or we shall both repent it.
Frown quickly, then, and break my heart,
  That so my way of dying
May, though my life was full of smart,
  Be worth the world's envỳing.

Some, striving knowledge to refine,
  Consume themselves with thinking;
And some who friendship seal in wine
  Are kindly killed with drinking;
And some are wrecked on the Indian coast,
  Thither by gain invited;
Some are in smoke of battle lost,
  Whom drums, not lutes, delighted.

Alas! how poorly these depart,
  Their graves still unattended;
Who dies not of a broken heart
  Is not of Death commended.
His memory is only sweet,
  All praise and pity moving,
Who kindly at his mistress' feet
  Does die with over-loving.

SPENSER TO MILTON

SONG

J. MILTON

O'ER the smooth enamelled green
Where no print of step hath been,
    Follow me, as I sing
    And touch the warbled string,
Under the shady roof
Of branching elm star-proof,
    Follow me.
I will bring you where she sits
Clad in splendour as befits
    Her deity.
Such a rural Queen
All Arcadia hath not seen.

Nymphs and Shepherds, dance no more
    By sandy Ladon's lilied banks,
On old Lycæus or Cyllene hoar
    Trip no more in twilight ranks;
Though Erymanth your loss deplore,
    A better soil shall give ye thanks.
From the stony Mænalus
Bring your flocks, and live with us;
Here ye shall have greater grace,
To serve the Lady of this place.
Though Syrinx your Pan's mistress were
Yet Syrinx well might wait on her.
        Such a rural Queen
        All Arcadia hath not seen.

SONG OF THE PRIEST OF PAN

J. FLETCHER

SHEPHERDS all, and maidens fair,
Fold your flocks up, for the air
'Gins to thicken, and the sun
Already his great course hath run.
See the dew-drops how they kiss
Every little flower that is,
Hanging on their velvet heads,
Like a rope of crystal beads:
See the heavy clouds low falling,
And bright Hesperus down calling
The dead Night from under ground;
At whose rising, mists unsound,
Damps and vapours fly apace,
Hovering o'er the wanton face
Of these pastures, where they come,
Striking dead both bud and bloom:
Therefore, from such danger lock
Every one his lovèd flock;
And let your dogs lie loose without,
Lest the wolf come as a scout
From the mountain, and, ere day,
Bear a lamb or kid away;
Or the crafty thievish fox
Break upon your simple flocks.
To secure yourselves from these,
Be not too secure in ease;
Let one eye his watches keep,
Whilst the other eye doth sleep;
So you shall good shepherds prove,
And for ever hold the love
Of our great god. Sweetest slumbers
And soft silence, fall in numbers
On your eyelids! So, farewell!
Thus I end my evening's knell.

SPENSER TO MILTON

HENCE WITH PASSION

T. HEYWOOD

HENCE with passion, sighs and tears,
Disasters, sorrows, cares and fears!
See my Love, my Love, appears,
  That thought himself exiled!
Whence might all these loud joys grow,
Whence might mirth and banquets flow,
But that he 's come, he 's come, I know?
  Fair Fortune, thou hast smiled.

Give unto these windows eyes,
Daze the stars and mock the skies,
And let us two, us two, devise
  To lavish our best treasures;
Crown our wishes with content,
Meet our souls in sweet consent,
And let this night, this night, be spent
  In all abundant pleasures.

THE SHEPHERD'S LAY

W. BROWNE

SHALL I tell you whom I love?
  Hearken then awhile to me;
And if such a woman move
  As I now shall versify,
Be assured 'tis she, or none,
That I love, and love alone.

Nature did her so much right
  As she scorns the help of art,
In as many virtues dight
  As e'er yet embraced a heart:

So much good, so truly tried,
Some for less were deified.

Wit she hath, without desire
  To make known how much she hath;
And her anger flames no higher
  Than may fitly sweeten wrath,
Full of pity as may be,
Though perhaps not so to me.

Reason masters every sense;
  And her virtues grace her birth;
Lovely as all excellence,
  Modest in her most of mirth:
Likelihood enough to prove
Only worth could kindle love.

Such she is: and if you know
  Such a one as I have sung,
Be she brown, or fair, or so
  That she be but somewhile young;
Be assured 'tis she, or none,
That I love, and love alone.

THE NIGHTINGALE

R. BARNEFIELD

As it fell upon a day
In the merry month of May,
Sitting in a pleasant shade
Which a grove of myrtles made,
Beasts did leap and birds did sing,
Trees did grow and plants did spring;
Everything did banish moan
Save the Nightingale alone:
She, poor bird as all forlorn
Leaned her breast against a thorn,

And there sung the dolefull'st ditty,
That to hear it was great pity.
Fie, fie, fie! now would she cry;
Tereu, Tereu! by and by;
That to hear her so complain
Scarce I could from tears refrain;
For her griefs so lively shown
Made me think upon mine own.
Ah! thought I, thou mourn'st in vain,
None takes pity on thy pain:
Senseless trees they cannot hear thee,
Ruthless beasts they will not cheer thee:
King Pandion, he is dead,
All thy friends are lapped in lead;
All thy fellow birds do sing
Careless of thy sorrowing:
Even so, poor bird, like thee,
None alive will pity me.

BEAUTY'S SELF

ANON.

MY Love in her attire doth show her wit,
  It doth so well become her ;
For every season she hath dressings fit,
  For Winter, Spring, and Summer.
    No beauty she doth miss
      When all her robes are on :
    But Beauty's self she is
      When all her robes are gone.

SONG

W. SHAKESPEARE

ORPHEUS with his lute made trees
And the mountain tops that freeze
  Bow themselves when he did sing :
To his music, plants and flowers
Ever sprung ; as sun and showers
  There had made a lasting spring.

Every thing that heard him play,
Even the billows of the sea,
  Hung their heads and then lay by,—
In sweet music is such art,
Killing care and grief of heart,
  Fall asleep, or hearing, die.

SPENSER TO MILTON

THERE IS A LADY SWEET AND KIND

ANON.

THERE is a Lady sweet and kind,
Was never face so pleased my mind;
I did but see her passing by,
And yet I love her till I die.

Her gesture, motion, and her smiles,
Her wit, her voice my heart beguiles,
Beguiles my heart, I know not why,
And yet I love her till I die.

Cupid is wingèd and doth range;
Her country so my love doth change,—
But change she earth, or change she sky,
Yet will I love her till I die.

ELIZABETH OF BOHEMIA

SIR H. WOTTON

YOU meaner beauties of the night,
  That poorly satisfy our eyes
More by your number than your light,
  You common people of the skies;
What are you when the Moon shall rise?

You curious chanters of the wood
  That warble forth Dame Nature's lays,
Thinking your passions understood
  By your weak accents; what's your praise
When Philomel her voice shall raise?

You violets that first appear
  By your pure purple mantles known,
Like the proud virgins of the year,
  As if the spring were all your own;
What are you when the Rose is blown?

So, when my Mistress shall be seen
  In sweetness of her looks and mind,
By virtue first, then choice, a Queen,
  Tell me, if she were not designed
Th' eclipse and glory of her kind?

BEAUTY BATHING

A. MUNDAY

BEAUTY sat bathing by a spring,
  Where fairest shades did hide her;
The winds blew calm, the birds did sing,
  The cool streams ran beside her.
My wanton thoughts enticed mine eye
  To see what was forbidden:
But better memory said Fie;
  So vain desire was chidden—
      Hey nonny nonny O!
      Hey nonny nonny!

Into a slumber then I fell,
  And fond imagination
Seemèd to see, but could not tell,
  Her feature or her fashion:
But ev'n as babes in dreams do smile,
  And sometimes fall a-weeping,
So I awaked as wise this while
  As when I fell a-sleeping.
      Hey nonny nonny O!
      Hey nonny nonny!

SPENSER TO MILTON

CHARIS'S TRIUMPH

B. JONSON

SEE the chariot at hand here of Love,
  Wherein my Lady rideth!
Each that draws is a swan or a dove,
  And well the car Love guideth.
As she goes, all hearts do duty
          Unto her beauty;
And enamoured do wish, so they might
          But enjoy such a sight,
That they still were to run by her side,
Through swords, through seas, whither she would ride.

Do but look on her eyes, they do light
  All that Love's world compriseth!
Do but look on her hair, it is bright
  As Love's star when it riseth!
Do but mark—her forehead 's smoother
          Than words that soothe her;
And from her arched brows, such a grace
          Sheds itself through the face,
As alone there triumphs to the life
All the gain, all the good, of the elements' strife.

Have you seen but a bright lily grow
  Before rude hands have touched it?
Have you marked but the fall of the snow
  Before the soil hath smutched it?
Have you felt the wool of the beaver,
          Or swan's down ever?
Or have smelt o' the bud o' the brier,
          Or the nard in the fire?
Or have tasted the bag of the bee?
O so white, O so soft, O so sweet is she!

WHERE THE BEE SUCKS

W. SHAKESPEARE

WHERE the bee sucks, there suck I;
In a cowslip's bell I lie:
There I couch when owls do cry.
On the bat's back I do fly
After summer merrily:
  Merrily, merrily, shall I live now,
  Under the blossom that hangs on the bough.

OVER HILL, OVER DALE

W. SHAKESPEARE

  OVER hill, over dale,
    Thorough bush, thorough brier,
  Over park, over pale,
    Thorough flood, thorough fire,
  I do wander everywhere,
  Swifter than the moon's sphere;
  And I serve the fairy Queen,
  To dew her orbs upon the green:
  The cowslips tall her pensioners be;
  In their gold coats spots you see;
  Those be rubies, fairy favours,
  In those freckles live their savours:
I must go seek some dew-drops here,
And hang a pearl in every cowslip's ear.

OVER HILL, OVER DALE, THOROUGH BUSH, THOROUGH BRIER
OVER PARK, OVER PALE, THOROUGH FLOOD, THOROUGH FIRE

SPENSER TO MILTON

TITANIA

W. SHAKESPEARE

YOU spotted snakes, with double tongue,
  Thorny hedgehogs, be not seen;
Newts and blind-worms, do no wrong;
  Come not near our fairy queen.

    Philomel, with melody
    Sing in our sweet lullaby;
  Lulla, lulla, lullaby; lulla, lulla, lullaby:
      Never harm,
      Nor spell nor charm,
    Come our lovely lady nigh;
    So, good night, with lullaby.

Weaving spiders, come not here;
  Hence, you long-legged spinners, hence!
Beetles black, approach not near;
  Worm, nor snail, do no offence.

    Philomel, with melody
    Sing in our sweet lullaby;
  Lulla, lulla, lullaby; lulla, lulla, lullaby:
      Never harm,
      Nor spell nor charm,
    Come our lovely lady nigh;
    So, good night, with lullaby.

JACK AND JOAN

T. CAMPION

JACK and Joan, they think no ill,
But loving live, and merry still;
Do their week-days' work, and pray
Devoutly on the holy-day:
Skip and trip it on the green,
And help to choose the Summer Queen;
Lash out at a country feast
Their silver penny with the best.

Well can they judge of nappy ale,
And tell at large a winter tale;
Climb up to the apple loft,
And turn the crabs till they be soft.
Tib is all the father's joy,
And little Tom the mother's boy:—
All their pleasure is, Content,
And care, to pay their yearly rent.

Joan can call by name her cows
And deck her windows with green boughs;
She can wreaths and tutties[1] make,
And trim with plums a bridal cake.
Jack knows what brings gain or loss,
And his long flail can stoutly toss:
Makes the hedge which others break,
And ever thinks what he doth speak.

—Now, you courtly dames and knights,
That study only strange delights,
Though you scorn the homespun gray,
And revel in your rich array;
Though your tongues dissemble deep
And can your heads from danger keep;
Yet, for all your pomp and train,
Securer lives the silly swain!

[1] Nosegays.

SPENSER TO MILTON

PUCK'S SONG

W. SHAKESPEARE

Now the hungry lion roars,
  And the wolf behowls the moon;
Whilst the heavy ploughman snores,
  All with weary task fordone.
Now the wasted brands do glow,
  Whilst the screech-owl, screeching loud,
Puts the wretch, that lies in woe,
  In remembrance of a shroud.
Now it is the time of night,
  That the graves, all gaping wide,
Every one lets forth his sprite,
  In the church-way paths to glide:
And we fairies that do run
  By the triple Hecate's team,
From the presence of the sun,
  Following darkness like a dream,
Now are frolic; not a mouse
Shall disturb this hallowed house:
I am sent, with broom before,
To sweep the dust behind the door.

TELL ME WHERE IS FANCY BRED

W. SHAKESPEARE

TELL me where is Fancy bred,
Or in the heart or in the head?
How begot, how nourishèd?
    Reply, reply.
It is engendered in the eyes,
With gazing fed; and Fancy dies
In the cradle where it lies.
    Let us all ring Fancy's knell:
    I'll begin it,—Ding, dong, bell.
Ding dong, bell.

THE WAKE

R. HERRICK

COME, Anthea, let us two
Go to feast, as others do.
Tarts and custards, creams and cakes,
Are the junkets still at wakes;
Unto which the tribes resort,
Where the business is the sport.
Morris-dancers thou shalt see;
Marian, too, in pageantry,
And a mimic to devise
Many grinning properties.
Players there will be, and those
Base in action as in clothes;
Yet with strutting they will please
The incurious villages.
Near the dying of the day,
There will be a cudgel-play,
Where a coxcomb will be broke,
Ere a good word can be spoke;
But the anger ends all here,
Drenched in ale, or drowned in beer.
Happy rustics! best content
With the cheapest merriment;
And possess no other fear,
Than to want the Wake next year.

SPENSER TO MILTON

BEGGARS' HOLIDAY SONG

J. FLETCHER

Cast our caps and cares away,
This is beggars' holiday!
At the crowning of our king
Thus we ever dance and sing.
In the world look out and see
Where 's so happy a prince as he?
Where the nation lives so free,
And so merry as do we?
Be it peace, or be it war,
Here at liberty we are,
And enjoy our ease and rest;
To the field we are not pressed,
Nor are called into the town
To be troubled with the gown.
Hang all offices, we cry,
And the magistrate too, by.
When the subsidy 's increased
We are not a penny sessed,
Nor will any go to law
With the beggar for a straw.
All which happiness, he brags
He doth owe unto his rags.

DEAR, IF YOU CHANGE, I'LL NEVER CHOOSE AGAIN

ANON.

DEAR, if you change, I'll never choose again ;
Sweet, if you shrink, I'll never think of love ;
Fair, if you fail, I'll judge all beauty vain ;
Wise, if too weak, more wits I'll never prove.
Dear, sweet, fair, wise ! change, shrink, nor be not weak ;
And, on my faith, my faith shall never break.

Earth with her flowers shall sooner heaven adorn ;
Heaven her bright stars through earth's dim globe shall move :
Fire heat shall lose, and frosts of flames be born ;
Air, made to shine, as black as hell shall prove :
Earth, heaven, fire, air, the world transformed shall view,
Ere I prove false to faith or strange to you.

SONNET

M. DRAYTON

SINCE there 's no help, come let us kiss and part—
Nay, I have done, you get no more of me ;
And I am glad, yea, glad with all my heart,
That thus so cleanly I myself can free ;
Shake hands for ever, cancel all our vows,
And when we meet at any time again,
Be it not seen in either of our brows
That we one jot of former love retain.
Now at the last gasp of Love's latest breath,
When, his pulse failing, Passion speechless lies,
When Faith is kneeling by his bed of death,
And Innocence is closing up his eyes,
—Now if thou wouldst, when all have given him over,
From death to life thou mightst him yet recover !

SPENSER TO MILTON

SONG

J. DONNE

SWEETEST love, I do not go
For weariness of thee,
Nor in hope the world can show
A fitter love for me;
But since that I
At the last must part, 'tis best
Thus to use myself in jest
By feignèd deaths to die.

Yesternight the sun went hence,
And yet is here to-day;
He hath no desire nor sense,
Nor half so short a way:
Then fear not me,
But believe that I shall make
Speedier journeys, since I take
More wings and spurs than he.

O how feeble is man's pow'r!
That if good fortune fall,
Cannot add another hour,
Nor a lost hour recall;
But come bad chance,
And we join to it our strength,
And we teach it art and length
Itself o'er us to advance.

When thou sigh'st thou sigh'st not wind,
But sigh'st my soul away;
When thou weep'st, unkindly kind,
My life's blood doth decay.
It cannot be
That thou lovest me as thou say'st
If in thine my life thou waste,
That art the best of me.

Let not thy divining heart
Forethink me any ill;
Destiny may take thy part
And may thy fears fulfil;
But think that we
Are but turned aside to sleep.
They who one another keep
Alive, ne'er parted be!

SAMELA

R. GREENE

LIKE to Diana in her summer weed,
Girt with a crimson robe of brightest dye,
Goes fair Samela.
Whiter than be the flocks that straggling feed
When washed by Arethusa fount they lie,
Is fair Samela.
As fair Aurora in her morning gray,
Decked with the ruddy glister of her love
Is fair Samela;
Like lovely Thetis on a calmèd day
Whenas her brightness Neptune's fancies move,
Shines fair Samela.
Her tresses gold, her eyes like glassy streams,
Her teeth are pearl, the breasts are ivory
Of fair Samela.
Her cheeks like rose and lily yield forth gleams;
Her brows bright arches framed of ebony:
Thus fair Samela
Passeth fair Venus in her bravest hue,
And Juno in the show of majesty:
For she's Samela.
Pallas in wit,—all three, if you will view,
For beauty, wit, and matchless dignity,
Yield to Samela.

SLEEP, ANGRY BEAUTY

T. CAMPION

SLEEP, angry beauty, sleep and fear not me!
  For who a sleeping lion dares provoke?
It shall suffice me here to sit and see
  Those lips shut up that never kindly spoke:
What sight can more content a lover's mind
Than beauty seeming harmless, if not kind?

My words have charmed her, for secure she sleeps,
  Though guilty much of wrong done to my love;
And in her slumber, see! she close-eyed weeps:
  Dreams often more than waking passions move.
Plead, Sleep, my cause, and make her soft like thee,
That she in peace may wake and pity me.

DIAPHENIA

H. CONSTABLE

DIAPHENIA like the daffadowndilly,
White as the sun, fair as the lily,
  Heigh ho, how I do love thee!
I do love thee as my lambs
Are belovèd of their dams—
  How blest were I if thou would'st prove me!

Diaphenia like the spreading roses,
That in thy sweets all sweets encloses,
  Fair sweet, how I do love thee!
I do love thee as each flower
Loves the sun's life-giving power
  For dead, thy breath to life might move me.

Diaphenia, like to all things blessèd
When all thy praises are expressèd,
  Dear joy, how I do love thee!
As the birds do love the spring,
Or the bees their careful king:
  Then in requite, sweet virgin, love me!

TO PHILLIS, THE FAIR SHEPHERDESS

SIR E. DYER

MY Phillis hath the morning sun
  At first to look upon her,
And Phillis hath morn-waking birds
  Her rising still to honour.
My Phillis hath prime feathered flowers
  That smile when she treads on them,
And Phillis hath a gallant flock
  That leaps since she doth own them.

DIAPHENIA LIKE THE DAFFADOWNDILLY
WHITE AS THE SUN, FAIR AS THE LILY

But Phillis hath too hard a heart,
  Alas, that she should have it!
It yields no mercy to desert
  Nor grace to those who crave it.
Sweet Sun, when thou look'st on,
Pray her regard my moan!
Sweet birds, when you sing to her
To yield some pity woo her!
Sweet flowers that she treads on,
Tell her, her beauty dreads one,
And if in life her love she nill agree me,
Pray her before I die, she will come see me.

SONNET

W. SHAKESPEARE

WHEN in disgrace with fortune and men's eyes
I all alone beweep my outcast state,
And trouble deaf heaven with my bootless cries,
And look upon myself, and curse my fate,
Wishing me like to one more rich in hope,
Featured like him, like him with friends possessed,
Desiring this man's art and that man's scope,
With what I most enjoy contented least;
Yet in these thoughts myself almost despising,—
Haply I think on Thee; and then my state,
Like to the lark at break of day arising
From sullen earth, sings hymns at heaven's gate;
For thy sweet love remembered such wealth brings
That then I scorn to change my state with kings.

FAREWELL, DEAR LOVE

ANON.

FAREWELL, dear love! since thou wilt needs be gone:
Mine eyes do show my life is almost done.
—Nay I will never die,
So long as I can spy;
There be many mo
Though that she do go.
There be many mo, I fear not;
Why, then, let her go, I care not.—

Farewell, farewell! since this I find is true,
I will not spend more time in wooing you.
—But I will seek elsewhere
If I may find her there.
Shall I bid her go?
What and if I do?
Shall I bid her go and spare not?
O no, no, no, no, I dare not.—

Ten thousand times farewell! yet stay awhile.
Sweet, kiss me once, sweet kisses time beguile.
—I have no power to move:
How now, am I in love?—
Wilt thou needs be gone?
Go then, all is one.
Wilt thou needs be gone? O hie thee!
Nay; stay, and do no more deny me.

Once more farewell! I see *Loth to depart*,[1]
Bids oft adieu to her that holds my heart:
But seeing I must lose
Thy love which I did choose,
Go thy ways for me,
Since it may not be:
Go thy ways for me, but whither?
Go,—oh, but where I may come thither.

[1] An old song with this title.

SPENSER TO MILTON

What shall I do? my love is now departed,
She is as fair as she is cruel-hearted:
　　She would not be entreated
　　With prayers oft repeated.
　　If she come no more,
　　Shall I die therefore?
If she come no more, what care I?
—Faith, let her go, or come, or tarry!

TO HIS COY LOVE

M. DRAYTON

I PRAY thee leave, love me no more,
　Call home the heart you gave me,
I but in vain that saint adore
　That can but will not save me.
These poor half kisses kill me quite;
　Was ever man thus served?
Amidst an ocean of delight
　For pleasure to be starved.

Show me no more those snowy breasts
　With azure riverets branched,
Where whilst mine eye with plenty feasts,
　Yet is my thirst not stanched.
O Tantalus, thy pains ne'er tell,
　By me thou art prevented;
'Tis nothing to be plagued in Hell,
　But thus in Heaven tormented.

Clip me no more in those dear arms,
　Nor thy life's comfort call me;
O these are but too powerful charms
　And do but more enthral me.
But see how patient I am grown
　In all this coil about thee;
Come, nice thing, let thy heart alone;
　I cannot live without thee.

COME AWAY, COME AWAY, DEATH

W. SHAKESPEARE

COME away, come away, Death,
And in sad cypress let me be laid;
Fly away, fly away, breath;
I am slain by a fair cruel maid.
My shroud of white, stuck all with yew,
O prepare it!
My part of death, no one so true
Did share it.

Not a flower, not a flower sweet,
On my black coffin let there be strown;
Not a friend, not a friend greet
My poor corpse, where my bones shall be thrown:
A thousand thousand sighs to save
Lay me, O, where
Sad true lover never find my grave
To weep there!

SHALL I, WASTING IN DESPAIR

G. WITHER

SHALL I, wasting in despair,
Die because a woman's fair?
Or my cheeks make pale with care
'Cause another's rosy are?
Be she fairer than the day,
Or the flowery meads in May—
If she be not so to me,
What care I how fair she be?

SPENSER TO MILTON

Shall my foolish heart be pined
'Cause I see a woman kind?
Or a well disposèd nature
Joinèd with a lovely feature?
Be she meeker, kinder, than
Turtle-dove or pelican,
   If she be not so to me,
   What care I how kind she be?

Shall a woman's virtues move
Me to perish for her love?
Or her well-deservings known
Make me quite forget mine own?
Be she with that goodness blest
Which may gain her name of Best;
   If she seem not such to me,
   What care I how good she be?

'Cause her fortune seems too high,
Shall I play the fool and die?
She that bears a noble mind,
If not outward helps she find,
Thinks what with them he would do
Who without them dares to woo;
   And unless that mind I see,
   What care I how great she be?

Great, or good, or kind, or fair,
I will ne'er the more despair;
If she love me, this believe,
I will die ere she shall grieve;
If she slight me when I woo,
I can scorn and let her go;
   For if she be not for me,
   What care I for whom she be?

THE FAITHLESS SHEPHERDESS

ANON.

WHILE that the sun with his beams hot
  Scorchèd the fruits in vale and mountain,
Philon the shepherd, late forgot,
  Sitting beside a crystal fountain
    In shadow of a green oak tree,
    Upon his pipe this song played he:
Adieu, Love, adieu, Love, untrue Love!
Untrue Love, untrue Love, adieu, Love!
Your mind is light, soon lost for new love.

So long as I was in your sight
  I was your heart, your soul, your treasure;
And evermore you sobbed and sighed
  Burning in flames beyond all measure:
    —Three days endured your love to me,
    And it was lost in other three!
Adieu, Love, adieu, Love, untrue Love!
Untrue Love, untrue Love, adieu, Love!
Your mind is light, soon lost for new love.

Another shepherd you did see
  To whom your heart was soon enchainèd;
Full soon your love was leapt from me,
  Full soon my place he had obtainèd.
    Soon came a third your love to win,
    And we were out and he was in.
Adieu, Love, adieu, Love, untrue Love!
Untrue Love, untrue Love, adieu, Love!
Your mind is light, soon lost for new love.

SPENSER TO MILTON

Sure you have made me passing glad
  That you your mind so soon removèd,
Before that I the leisure had
  To choose you for my best belovèd :
    For all my love was past and done
    Two days before it was begun ;—
Adieu, Love, adieu, Love, untrue Love
Untrue Love, untrue Love, adieu, Love!
Your mind is light, soon lost for new love.

A FAREWELL TO AN UNKIND MISTRESS

F. DAVISON

SWEET, if you like and love me still,
And yield me love for my good will,
And do not from your promise start,
When your fair hand gave me your heart ;
  If dear to you I be,
  As you are dear to me ;
Then yours I am and will be ever,
Nor time nor place my love shall sever ;
But faithful still I will presever,
  Like constant marble stone,
  Loving but you alone.

But if you favour more than me,
Who love thee dear and none but thee ;
If others do the harvest gain,
That 's due to me for all my pain ;
  If you delight to range,
  And oft to chop and change ;
Then get you some new-fangled mate,
My doting love shall turn to hate,
Esteeming you, though too, too late
  Not worth a pebble stone,
  Loving not me alone.

TO HIS FORSAKEN MISTRESS

SIR R. AYTON

I DO confess thou'rt smooth and fair,
  And I might have gone near to love thee,
Had I not found the slightest prayer
  That lips could speak, had power to move thee ;
But I can let thee now alone
As worthy to be loved by none.

I do confess thou'rt sweet ; yet find
  Thee such an unthrift of thy sweets,
Thy favours are but like the wind
  That kisseth everything it meets :
And since thou canst with more than one,
Thou'rt worthy to be kissed by none.

The morning rose that untouched stands
  Armed with her briars, how sweet she smells !
But plucked and strained through ruder hands,
  Her scent no longer with her dwells :
But scent and beauty both are gone,
And leaves fall from her, one by one.

Such fate ere long will thee betide
  When thou hast handled been awhile,
With sere flowers to be thrown aside ;—
  And I shall sigh, while some will smile,
To see thy love for more than one
Hath brought thee to be loved by none.

ENCOURAGEMENTS TO A LOVER

SIR J. SUCKLING

WHY so pale and wan, fond lover?
Prythee, why so pale?
Will, if looking well can't move her,
Looking ill prevail?
Prythee, why so pale?

Why so dull and mute, young sinner?
Prythee, why so mute?
Will, when speaking well can't win her,
Saying nothing do 't?
Prythee, why so mute?

Quit, quit, for shame! this will not move,
This cannot take her;
If of herself she will not love,
Nothing can make her:
The D—l take her!

FIRE THAT MUST FLAME

T. CAMPION

FIRE that must flame is with apt fuel fed;
Flowers that will thrive in sunny soil are bred;
How can a heart feel heat that no hope finds?
Or can he love on whom no comfort shines?

Fair! I confess there's pleasure in your sight:
Sweet! you have power, I grant, of all delight:
But what is all to me, if I have none?
Churl that you are, t' enjoy such wealth alone!

Prayers move the heavens but find no grace with you;
Yet in your looks a heavenly form I view;
Then will I pray again, hoping to find,
As well as in your looks, Heaven in your mind.

Saint of my heart, Queen of my life and love,
O let my vows thy loving spirit move!
Let me no longer mourn through thy disdain;
But with one touch of grace cure all my pain!

TO HIS COY MISTRESS

A. MARVELL

HAD we but world enough and time,
This coyness, lady, were no crime.
We would sit down and think which way
To walk, and pass our long love's day.
Thou by the Indian Ganges' side
Shouldst rubies find: I by the tide
Of Humber would complain. I would
Love you ten years before the flood,
And you should, if you please, refuse
Till the conversion of the Jews.

SPENSER TO MILTON

My vegetable love should grow
Vaster than empires, and more slow;
An hundred years should go to praise
Thine eyes and on thy forehead gaze;
Two hundred to adore each breast,
But thirty thousand to the rest;
An age at least to every part,
And the last age should show your heart;
For, lady, you deserve this state,
Nor would I love at lower rate.

But at my back I always hear
Time's wingèd chariot hurrying near;
And yonder all before us lie
Deserts of vast eternity.
The grave's a fine and private place,
But none, I think, do there embrace.
Now therefore while the youthful hue
Sits on thy skin like morning dew,
And while thy willing soul transpires
At every pore with instant fires,
Now let us sport us while we may,
And now, like amorous birds of prey,
Rather at once our time devour
Than languish in his slow-chapt power.
Let us roll all our strength and all
Our sweetness up into one ball,
And tear our pleasures with rough strife
Thorough the iron gates of life:
Thus, though we cannot make our sun
Stand still, yet we will make him run.

THE SHEPHERD'S WIFE'S SONG

R. GREENE

AH, what is Love? It is a pretty thing,
As sweet unto a shepherd as a king;
And sweeter too;
For kings have cares that wait upon a crown,
And cares can make the sweetest love to frown:
Ah then, ah then,
If country loves such sweet desires do gain,
What lady would not love a shepherd swain?

His flocks are folded, he comes home at night,
As merry as a king in his delight;
And merrier too;
For kings bethink then what the state require,
Where shepherds careless carol by the fire:
Ah then, ah then,
If country loves such sweet desires do gain,
What lady would not love a shepherd swain?

He kisseth first, then sits as blithe to eat
His cream and curds as doth the king his meat;
And blither too;
For kings have often fears when they do sup,
Where shepherds dread no poison in their cup:
Ah then, ah then,
If country loves such sweet desires do gain,
What lady would not love a shepherd swain?

Upon his couch of straw he sleeps as sound
As doth a king upon his bed of down;
More sounder too;
For cares cause kings full oft their sleep to spill,
Where weary shepherds lie and snort their fill:
Ah then, ah then,
If country loves such sweet desires do gain,
What lady would not love a shepherd swain?

Thus with his wife he spends the year, as blithe
As doth the king at every tide or sithe;
    And blither too;
For kings have wars and broils to take in hand,
Where shepherds laugh and love upon the land:
    Ah then, ah then,
If country loves such sweet desires do gain,
What lady would not love a shepherd swain?

SONNET

E. SPENSER

ONE day I wrote her name upon the strand,
But came the waves and washèd it away:
Again I wrote it with a second hand,
But came the tide and made my pains his prey.
Vain man! said she, that dost in vain assay
A mortal thing so to immortalise;
For I myself shall like to this decay,
And eke my name be wipèd out likewise.
Not so, quoth I; let baser things devise
To die in dust, but you shall live by fame;
My verse your virtues rare shall eternise,
And in the heavens write your glorious name:
Where, whenas death shall all the world subdue,
Our love shall live, and later life renew.

CUPID IN A BED OF ROSES

ANON.

CUPID, in a bed of roses
Sleeping, chanced to be stung
Of a bee that lay among
The flowers where he himself reposes;
And thus to his mother weeping
Told that he this wound did take
Of a little wingèd snake,
As he lay securely sleeping.
Cytherea smiling said
That "if so great sorrow spring
From a silly bee's weak sting
As should make thee thus dismayed,
What anguish feel they, think'st thou, and what pain
Whom thy empoisoned arrows cause complain?"

VENUS AND ADONIS

W. BROWNE

VENUS by Adonis' side
Crying kissed and kissing cried,
Wrung her hands and tore her hair
For Adonis dying there.

Stay, quoth she, O stay and live!
Nature surely doth not give
To the earth her sweetest flowers
To be seen but some few hours.

On his face still as he bled
For each drop a tear she shed,
Which she kissed or wiped away,
Else had drowned him where he lay.

CUPID IN A BED OF ROSES

SPENSER TO MILTON

Fair Proserpina, quoth she,
Shall not have thee yet from me,
Nor thy soul to fly begin,
While my lips can keep it in.

Here she closed again. And some
Say Apollo would have come
To have cured his wounded limb,
But that she had smothered him.

HEAR, YE LADIES THAT DESPISE

J. FLETCHER

HEAR, ye ladies that despise,
What the mighty Love has done:
Fear examples and be wise.
Fair Calisto was a nun;
Leda sailing on the stream
To deceive the hopes of man,
Love accounting but a dream,
Doted on a silver swan;
Danaë in a brazen tower
Where no love was, loved a shower.

Hear, ye ladies that are coy,
What the mighty Love can do:
Fear the fierceness of the boy.
The chaste moon he made to woo;
Vesta, kindling holy fires,
Circled round about with spies,
Never dreaming loose desires,
Doting at the altar dies;
Ilion, in a short hour, higher
He can build, and once more fire.

THERE IS A GARDEN IN HER FACE

T. CAMPION

THERE is a garden in her face
  Where roses and white lilies blow;
A heavenly paradise is that place
  Wherein all pleasant fruits do flow:
    There cherries grow that none may buy
    Till "Cherry-ripe" themselves do cry.

Those cherries fairly do enclose
  Of orient pearl a double row,
Which when her lovely laughter shows,
  They look like rose-buds filled with snow;
    Yet them nor peer nor prince can buy
    Till "Cherry-ripe" themselves do cry.

Her eyes like angels watch them still;
  Her brows like bended bows do stand,
Threatening with piercing frowns to kill
  All that attempt with eye or hand
    Those sacred cherries to come nigh,
    Till "Cherry-ripe" themselves do cry.

CHERRY-RIPE

R. HERRICK

CHERRY-RIPE, ripe, ripe, I cry,
Full and fair ones; come and buy.
If so be you ask me where
They do grow, I answer: There
Where my Julia's lips do smile;
There 's the land, or cherry-isle,
Whose plantations fully show
All the year where cherries grow.

SPENSER TO MILTON

TO HIS LOVE

MARQUIS OF MONTROSE

My dear and only Love, I pray
  This little world of thee
Be governed by no other sway
  But purest monarchy;
For if confusion have a part,
  Which virtuous souls abhor,
And hold a synod in thy heart,
  I'll never love thee more.

As Alexander I will reign,
  And I will reign alone;
My thoughts did evermore disdain
  A rival on my throne.
He either fears his fate too much,
  Or his deserts are small,
That dares not put it to the touch,
  To win or lose it all.

But I will reign and govern still
  And always give the law,
And have each subject at my will,
  And all to stand in awe;
But 'gainst my batteries if I find
  Thou storm, or vex me sore,
As if thou set me as a blind,
  I'll never love thee more.

But if thou wilt be constant then
  And faithful to thy word,
I'll make thee famous by my pen
  And glorious by my sword;

I'll serve thee in such noble ways
  Was never heard before;
I'll deck and crown thy head with bays,
  And love thee more and more.

THE QUEEN OF PAPHOS, ERYCINE

ANON.

THE Queen of Paphos, Erycine,
  In heart did rose-cheeked Adon love;
He mortal was, but she divine,
  And oft with kisses did him move;
With great gifts still she did him woo,
But he would never yield thereto.

Then since the Queen of Love by love
  To love was once a subject made,
And could thereof no pleasure prove,
  By day, by night, by light or shade,
Why, being mortal, should I grieve,
Since she herself could not relieve?

She was a goddess heavenly
  And loved a fair-faced earthly boy,
Who did contemn her deity
  And would not grant her hope of joy;
For Love doth govern by a fate
That here plants will and there leaves hate.

But I a hapless mortal wight
  To an immortal beauty sue;
No marvel then she loathes my sight
  Since Adon Venus would not woo.
Hence groaning sighs, mirth be my friend!
Before my life, my love shall end.

THE QUEEN OF PAPHOS, ERYCINE
IN HEART DID ROSE-CHEEKED ADON LOVE

SPENSER TO MILTON

WISHES TO HIS SUPPOSED MISTRESS

R. CRASHAW

WHOE'ER she be
That not impossible She
That shall command my heart and me ;

Where'er she lie,
Locked up from mortal eye
In shady leaves of destiny ;

Till that ripe birth
Of studied Fate step forth
And teach her fair steps tread our earth ;

Till that divine
Idea take a shrine
Of crystal flesh, through which to shine ;

Meet you her, my Wishes,
Bespeak her to my blisses,
And be ye called my absent kisses.

I wish her Beauty,
That owes not all its duty
To gaudy tire, or glist'ring shoe-tie.

A Face, that 's best
By its own beauty drest,
And can alone command the rest.

A Cheek, where youth
And blood, with pen of truth,
Write what the reader sweetly ru'th.

Lips, where all day
A lover's kiss may play,
Yet carry nothing thence away.

Eyes, that displace
The neighbour diamond, and outface
That sunshine by their own sweet grace.

Tresses, that wear
Jewels but to declare
How much themselves more precious are :

Whose native ray
Can tame the wanton day
Of gems that in their bright shades play.

A well tamed Heart,
For whose more noble smart
Love may be long choosing a dart.

Whate'er delight
Can make day's forehead bright,
Or give down to the wings of night.

Days that need borrow
No part of their good morrow,
From a fore-spent night of sorrow :

Days that, in spite
Of darkness, by the light
Of a clear mind are day all night.

Life that dares send
A challenge to his end,
And when it comes, say, "Welcome, friend !"

I wish her store
Of worth may leave her poor
Of wishes ; and I wish—no more.

SPENSER TO MILTON

Now, if Time knows
That Her, whose radiant brows
Weave them a garland of my vows;

Her that dares be
What these lines wish to see;
I seek no further, it is She.

TO ALTHEA FROM PRISON

R. LOVELACE

WHEN Love with unconfinèd wings
  Hovers within my gates,
And my divine Althea brings
  To whisper at the grates;
When I lie tangled in her hair
  And fettered to her eye,
The gods that wanton in the air
  Know no such liberty.

When flowing cups run swiftly round
  With no allaying Thames,
Our careless heads with roses crowned,
  Our hearts with loyal flames;
When thirsty grief in wine we steep,
  When healths and draughts go free—
Fishes that tipple in the deep
  Know no such liberty.

When, linnet-like confinèd, I
  With shriller throat shall sing
The sweetness, mercy, majesty
  And glories of my King;

When I shall voice aloud how good
He is, how great should be,
Enlargèd winds, that curl the flood,
Know no such liberty.

Stone walls do not a prison make,
Nor iron bars a cage;
Minds innocent and quiet take
That for an hermitage;
If I have freedom in my love
And in my soul am free,
Angels alone, that soar above,
Enjoy such liberty.

TO LUCASTA, ON GOING TO THE WARS

R. LOVELACE

TELL me not, Sweet, I am unkind
That from the nunnery
Of thy chaste breast and quiet mind,
To war and arms I fly.

True, a new mistress now I chase,
The first foe in the field;
And with a stronger faith embrace
A sword, a horse, a shield.

Yet this inconstancy is such
As you too shall adore;
I could not love thee, Dear, so much,
Loved I not Honour more.

SPENSER TO MILTON

A CAVALIER WAR-SONG

ANON.

A STEED, a steed, of matchless speed,
  A sword of metal keen ;
All else to noble hearts is dross,
  All else on earth is mean.
The neighing of the war-horse proud,
  The rolling of the drum,
The clangour of the trumpet loud,
  Be sounds from heaven that come.
And oh! the thundering press of knights,
  Whenas their war-cries swell,
May toll from heaven an angel bright,
  And rouse a fiend from hell.

Then mount, then mount, brave gallants all
  And don your helms amain ;
Death's couriers, Fame and Honour, call
  Us to the field again.
No shrewish tears shall fill our eye,
  When the sword-hilt 's in our hand ;
Heart-whole we'll part, and no whit sigh
  For the fairest in the land.
Let piping swain and craven wight
  Thus weep and puling cry ;
Our business is like men to fight,
  And, like to heroes, die!

THE COUNTRY LIFE

R. HERRICK

SWEET Country Life, to such unknown
Whose lives are others', not their own.
But, serving courts and cities, be
Less happy, less enjoying thee :—
Thou never plough'st the ocean's foam
To seek and bring rough pepper home ;
Nor to the Eastern Ind dost rove
To bring from thence the scorchèd clove ;
Nor, with the loss of thy loved rest,
Bring'st home the ingot from the West :
No ! thy ambition's masterpiece
Flies no thought higher than a fleece ;
Or how to pay thy hinds, and clear
All scores, and so to end the year :
But walk'st about thine own dear bounds,
Not envying others' larger grounds ;
For well thou know'st 'tis not th' extent
Of land makes life, but sweet content.
When now the cock, the ploughman's horn
Calls forth the lily-wristed morn,

Then to thy cornfields thou dost go,
Which though well soiled, yet thou dost know
That the best compost for the lands
Is the wise master's feet and hands:
There at the plough thou find'st thy team,
With a hind whistling there to them;
And cheer'st them up, by singing how
The kingdom's portion is the plough:
This done, then to th' enamelled meads
Thou go'st, and as thy foot there treads,
Thou seest a present God-like power
Imprinted in each herb and flower;
And smell'st the breath of great-eyed kine,
Sweet as the blossoms of the vine:
Here thou behold'st thy large sleek neat
Unto the dew-laps up in meat;
And as thou look'st, the wanton steer,
The heifer, cow, and ox draw near,
To make a pleasing pastime there:—
These seen, thou go'st to view thy flocks
Of sheep, safe from the wolf and fox,
And find'st their bellies there as full
Of short sweet grass, as backs with wool;
And leav'st them, as they feed and fill,
A shepherd piping on a hill.
For sports, for pageantry and plays,
Thou hast thy eves and holydays;
On which the young men and maids meet
To exercise their dancing feet,
Tripping the comely country round,
With daffodils and daisies crowned.
Thy wakes, thy quintels, here thou hast,
Thy May-poles too with garlands graced,
Thy morris-dance, thy Whitsun-ale,
Thy shearing-feasts, which never fail,
Thy harvest home, thy wassail bowl,
That 's tossed up after Fox' i' th' hole,

Thy mummeries, thy Twelfth-tide kings
And queens, thy Christmas revellings,—
Thy nut-brown mirth, thy russet wit,
And no man pays too dear for it:—
To these, thou hast thy times to go
And trace the hare i' th' treacherous snow:
Thy witty wiles to draw, and get
The lark into the trammel net;
Thou hast thy cock-rood and thy glade
To take the precious pheasant made;
Thy lime-twigs, snares, and pitfalls then
To catch the pilfering birds, not men.

O happy life! if that their good
The husbandmen but understood;
Who all the day themselves do please
And younglings, with such sports as these;
And, lying down, have nought t' affright
Sweet sleep, that makes more short the night.

SPENSER TO MILTON

THE GARDEN

A. MARVELL

HOW vainly men themselves amaze
To win the palm, the oak, or bays,
And their uncessant labours see
Crowned from some single herb or tree,
Whose short and narrow-vergèd shade
Does prudently their toils upbraid;
While all the flowers and trees do close
To weave the garlands of repose.

Fair Quiet, have I found thee here,
And Innocence thy sister dear!
Mistaken long, I sought you then
In busy companies of men:
Your sacred plants, if here below,
Only among the plants will grow:
Society is all but rude
To this delicious solitude.

No white nor red was ever seen
So amorous as this lovely green.
Fond lovers, cruel as their flame,
Cut in these trees their mistress' name:
Little, alas, they know or heed
How far these beauties her's exceed!
Fair trees! wheres'e'er your barks I wound,
No name shall but your own be found.

When we have run our passion's heat
Love hither makes his best retreat:
The gods, that mortal beauty chase,
Still in a tree did end their race;
Apollo hunted Daphne so
Only that she might laurel grow;

And Pan did after Syrinx speed
Not as a nymph, but for a reed.

What wondrous life is this I lead!
Ripe apples drop about my head;
The luscious clusters of the vine
Upon my mouth do crush their wine;
The nectarine and curious peach
Into my hands themselves do reach;
Stumbling on melons, as I pass,
Ensnared with flowers, I fall on grass.

Meanwhile the mind from pleasure less
Withdraws into its happiness;
The mind, that ocean where each kind
Does straight its own resemblance find;
Yet it creates, transcending these,
Far other worlds, and other seas;
Annihilating all that 's made
To a green thought in a green shade.

Here at the fountain's sliding foot
Or at some fruit-tree's mossy root,
Casting the body's vest aside
My soul into the boughs does glide;
There, like a bird, it sits and sings,
Then whets and combs its silver wings,
And, till prepared for longer flight,
Waves in its plumes the various light.

Such was that happy Garden-state
While man there walked without a mate:
After a place so pure and sweet,
What other help could yet be meet!
But 'twas beyond a mortal's share
To wander solitary there:
Two paradises 'twere in one,
To live in Paradise alone.

SPENSER TO MILTON

How well the skilful gardener drew
Of flowers and herbs this dial new!
Where, from above, the milder sun
Does through a fragrant zodiac run;
And, as it works, th' industrious bee
Computes its time as well as we!
How could such sweet and wholesome hours
Be reckoned, but with herbs and flowers?

CONTENT

R. GREENE

SWEET are the thoughts that savour of content;
  The quiet mind is richer than a crown;
Sweet are the nights in careless slumber spent;
  The poor estate scorns fortune's angry frown:
Such sweet content, such minds, such sleep, such bliss,
Beggars enjoy, when princes oft do miss.

The homely house that harbours quiet rest,
  The cottage that affords nor pride nor care,
The mean that 'grees with country music best,
  The sweet consort of mirth and modest fare;
Obscurèd life sets down a type of bliss:
A mind content both crown and kingdom is.

A WORLDLY PARADISE

N. BRETON

WHO can live in heart so glad
As the merry country lad?
Who upon a fair green balk
May at pleasure sit and walk,
And amid the azure skies
See the morning sun arise,—

While he hears in every spring
How the birds do chirp and sing:
Or before the hounds in cry
See the hare go stealing by:
Or along the shallow brook,
Angling with a baited hook,
See the fishes leap and play
In a blessèd sunny day:
Or to hear the partridge call,
Till she have her covey all:
Or to see the subtle fox,
How the villain plies the box;
After feeding on his prey,
How he closely sneaks away,
Through the hedge and down the furrow
Till he gets into his burrow:
Then the bee to gather honey,
And the little black-haired coney,
On a bank for sunny place,
With her forefeet wash her face:
Are not these, with thousands moe
Than the courts of kings do know,
The true pleasing spirit's sights
That may breed true love's delights?
But with all this happiness,
To behold that Shepherdess,
To whose eyes all shepherds yield
All the fairest of the field,
—Fair Aglaia, in whose face
Lives the shepherds' highest grace
For whose sake I say and swear,
By the passions that I bear,
Had I got a kingly grace,
I would leave my kingly place
And in heart be truly glad
To become a country lad;
Hard to lie, and go full bare,

And to feed on hungry fare,
So I might but live to be
Where I might but sit to see
Once a day, or all day long,
The sweet subject of my song:
In Aglaia's only eyes
All my worldly Paradise.

A CONTENTED MIND

J. SYLVESTER

I WEIGH not fortune's frown or smile;
 I joy not much in earthly joys;
I seek not state, I seek not style;
 I am not fond of fancy's toys;
I rest so pleased with what I have,
I wish no more, no more I crave.

I quake not at the thunder's crack;
 I tremble not at noise of war;
I swound not at the news of wrack;
 I shrink not at a blazing star;
I fear not loss, I hope not gain,
I envy none, I none disdain.

I see ambition never pleased;
 I see some Tantals starved in store;
I see gold's dropsy seldom eased;
 I see e'en Midas gape for more:
I neither want, nor yet abound—
Enough 's a feast, content is crowned.

I feign not friendship, where I hate;
 I fawn not on the great in show;
I prize, I praise a mean estate—
 Neither too lofty nor too low:
This, this is all my choice, my cheer—
A mind content, a conscience clear.

THE WISH

A. COWLEY

WELL then! I now do plainly see
This busy world and I shall ne'er agree.
The very honey of all earthly joy
Does of all meats the soonest cloy;
  And they, methinks, deserve my pity
Who for it can endure the stings,
The crowd, and buzz, and murmurings,
  Of this great hive, the City.

Ah! yet ere I descend to the grave,
May I a small house and large garden have;
And a few friends, and many books, both true,
Both wise, and both delightful too!
  And, since Love ne'er will from me flee,
A Mistress moderately fair,
And good as guardian angels are,
  Only beloved and loving me.

O fountains! when in you shall I
Myself eased of unpeaceful thoughts espy?
O fields! O woods! when, when shall I be made
The happy tenant of your shade?
  Here's the spring-head of pleasure's flood:
Here's wealthy Nature's treasury,
Where all the riches lie that she
  Has coined and stamped for good!

Pride and ambition here
Only in far-fetched metaphors appear;
Here nought but winds can hurtful murmurs scatter,
And nought but Echo flatter.
  The gods, when they descended, hither
From heaven, did always choose their way:
And therefore we may boldly say
  That 'tis the way too thither.

AND, SINCE LOVE NE'ER WILL FROM ME FLEE,
A MISTRESS MODERATELY FAIR

How happy here should I
And one dear She live, and embracing die!
She who is all the world, and can exclude
In deserts solitude.
  I should have then this only fear:
Lest men, when they my pleasures see,
Should hither throng to live like me;
  And so make a City here.

THE QUIET MIND

ANON.

I JOY not in no earthly bliss;
I force not Crœsus' wealth a straw;
For care I know not what it is;
I fear not Fortune's fatal law:
My mind is such as may not move
For beauty bright nor force of love.

I wish but what I have at will,
I wander not to seek for more.
I like the plain, I climb no hill;
In greatest storms, I sit on shore
And laugh at them that toil in vain
To get what must be lost again.

I kiss not where I wish to kill;
I feign not love where most I hate;
I break no sleep to win my will;
I wait not at the mighty's gate;
I scorn no poor, nor fear no rich;
I feel no want, nor have too much.

The court and cart I like nor loath.
Extremes are counted worst of all;
The golden mean, between them both
Doth surest sit and fears no fall.
This is my choice: for why? I find
No wealth is like the quiet mind.

MY MIND TO ME A KINGDOM IS

SIR E. DYER

My mind to me a kingdom is;
  Such present joys therein I find,
That it excels all other bliss
  That earth affords or grows by kind:
Though much I want that most would have,
Yet still my mind forbids to crave.

No princely pomp, no wealthy store,
  No force to win the victory,
No wily wit to salve a sore,
  No shape to feed a loving eye;
To none of these I yield as thrall;
For why? my mind doth serve for all.

I see how plenty surfeits oft,
  And hasty climbers soon do fall;
I see that those which are aloft
  Mishap doth threaten most of all:
They get with toil, they keep with fear:
Such cares my mind could never bear.

Content I live, this is my stay;
  I seek no more than may suffice;
I press to bear no haughty sway;
  Look, what I lack my mind supplies.
Lo, thus I triumph like a king,
Content with that my mind doth bring.

Some have too much, yet still do crave;
  I little have, and seek no more.
They are but poor, though much they have,
  And I am rich with little store;
They poor, I rich; they beg, I give;
They lack, I leave; they pine, I live.

SPENSER TO MILTON

I laugh not at another's loss,
  I grudge not at another 's gain;
No worldly waves my mind can toss;
  My state at one doth still remain:
I fear no foe, I fawn no friend;
I loathe not life, nor dread my end.

Some weigh their pleasure by their lust,
  Their wisdom by their rage of will;
Their treasure is their only trust,
  A cloakèd craft their store of skill:
But all the pleasure that I find
Is to maintain a quiet mind.

My wealth is health and perfect ease,
  My conscience clear my chief defence;
I neither seek by bribes to please,
  Nor by deceit to breed offence:
Thus do I live; thus will I die;
Would all did so as well as I!

THE MAN OF LIFE UPRIGHT

T. CAMPION

THE man of life upright,
  Whose guiltless heart is free
From all dishonest deeds,
  Or thought of vanity;

The man whose silent days
  In harmless joys are spent,
Whom hopes cannot delude,
  Nor sorrow discontent;

That man needs neither towers
  Nor armour for defence,
Nor secret vaults to fly
  From thunder's violence:

He only can behold
  With unaffrighted eyes
The horrors of the deep
  And terrors of the skies.

Thus, scorning all the cares
  That fate or fortune brings,
He makes the heaven his book,
  His wisdom heavenly things;

Good thoughts his only friends,
  His wealth a well-spent age,
The earth his sober inn
  And quiet pilgrimage.

CONTENT THYSELF WITH THY ESTATE

ANON.

CONTENT thyself with thy estate,
  Seek not to climb above the skies,
For often love is mixed with hate
  And 'twixt the flowers the serpent lies:
Where fortune sends her greatest joys,
There once possessed they are but toys.

What thing can earthly pleasure give
  That breeds delight when it is past?
Or who so quietly doth live
  But storms of care do drown at last?
This is the loan of worldly hire,
The more we have the more desire.

Wherefore I hold him best at ease
  That lives content with his estate,
And doth not sail in worldly seas
  Where Mine and Thine do breed debate:
This noble mind, even in a clown,
Is more than to possess a crown.

SPENSER TO MILTON

SWEET CONTENT

T. DEKKER

ART thou poor, yet hast thou golden slumbers?
O sweet content!
Art thou rich, yet is thy mind perplexed?
O punishment!
Dost thou laugh to see how fools are vexed
To add to golden numbers golden numbers?
O sweet content! O sweet, O sweet content!
Work apace, apace, apace, apace;
Honest labour bears a lovely face;
Then hey nonny nonny—hey nonny nonny!

Can'st drink the waters of the crispèd spring?
O sweet content!
Swim'st thou in wealth, yet sink'st in thine own tears?
O punishment!
Then he that patiently want's burden bears,
No burden bears, but is a king, a king!
O sweet content! O sweet, O sweet content!
Work apace, apace, apace, apace;
Honest labour bears a lovely face;
Then hey nonny nonny—hey nonny nonny!

IT IS NOT GROWING LIKE A TREE

B. JONSON

IT is not growing like a tree,
In bulk, doth make man better be;
Or standing long an oak, three hundred year,
To fall a log at last, dry, bald and sere:
A lily of a day
Is fairer far in May:
Although it fall and die that night,
It was the plant and flower of light.
In small proportions we just beauties see;
And in short measures life may perfect be.

ENGLISH LYRICS

THE GRASSHOPPER

A. COWLEY

HAPPY insect! what can be
In happiness compared to thee?
Fed with nourishment divine,
The dewy morning's gentle wine!
Nature waits upon thee still,
And thy verdant cup does fill;
'Tis filled wherever thou dost tread
Nature's self 's thy Ganymede.
Thou dost drink, and dance, and sing
Happier than the happiest king!
All the fields which thou dost see,
All the plants, belong to thee;
All that summer-hours produce,
Fertile made with early juice,
Man for thee does sow and plow;
Farmer he, and landlord thou!
Thou dost innocently joy,
Nor does thy luxury destroy.
The shepherd gladly heareth thee,
More harmonious than he.
Thee country hinds with gladness hear,
Prophet of the ripened year!
Thee Phœbus loves and does inspire;
Phœbus is himself thy sire;
To thee of all things upon earth
Life is no longer than thy mirth.
Happy insect! happy thou
Dost neither age nor winter know:
But when thou 'st drunk and danced and sung
Thy fill, the flow'ry leaves among,
(Voluptuous, and wise withal,
Epicurean animal!)
Sated with thy summer feast,
Thou retir'st to endless rest.

SPENSER TO MILTON

THE CHARACTER OF A HAPPY LIFE

SIR H. WOTTON

How happy is he born and taught
That serveth not another's will;
Whose armour is his honest thought,
And simple truth his utmost skill!

Whose passions not his masters are;
Whose soul is still prepared for death,
Not tied unto the world with care
Of public fame or private breath;

Who envies none that chance doth raise,
Nor vice; who never understood
How deepest wounds are given by praise;
Nor rules of state, but rules of good;

Who hath his life from rumours freed;
Whose conscience is his strong retreat;
Whose state can neither flatterers feed,
Nor ruin make oppressors great;

Who God doth late and early pray
More of His grace than gifts to lend;
And entertains the harmless day
With a religious book or friend;

—This man is freed from servile bands
Of hope to rise or fear to fall:
Lord of himself, though not of lands,
And having nothing, yet hath all.

DESIRE

ANON.

WHERE wit is over-ruled by will,
  And will is led by fond Desire,
There Reason were as good be still,
  As speaking, kindle greater fire;
For where Desire doth bear the sway,
The heart must rule, the head obey.

What boots the cunning pilot's skill,
  To tell which way to shape their course,
When he that steers will have his will,
  And drive them where he list, perforce?
So Reason shows the truth in vain,
Where fond Desire as king doth reign.

THE LIFE OF MAN

H. KING

LIKE to the falling of a star,
Or as the flights of eagles are,
Or like the fresh spring's gaudy hue,
Or silver drops of morning dew,
Or like a wind that chafes the flood,
Or bubbles which on water stood:
Even such is Man, whose borrowed light
Is straight called in and paid to night:
The wind blows out; the bubble dies;
The spring intombed in autumn lies;
The dew 's dried up; the star is shot;
The flight is past; and man forgot!

ANON.

WEEP you no more, sad fountains ;
What need you flow so fast ?
Look how the snowy mountains
Heaven's sun doth gently waste !
But my Sun's heavenly eyes
View not your weeping,
That now lies sleeping
Softly, now softly lies
Sleeping.

Sleep is a reconciling,
A rest that peace begets ;
Doth not the sun rise smiling
When fair at even he sets ?
Rest you then, rest, sad eyes !
Melt not in weeping
While she lies sleeping
Softly, now softly lies
Sleeping.

THE LAMENT

C. TICHBORNE

MY prime of youth is but a frost of cares;
  My feast of joy is but a dish of pain;
My crop of corn is but a field of tares;
  And all my good is but vain hope of gain;
The day is fled, and yet I saw no sun;
And now I live, and now my life is done!

The spring is past, and yet it hath not sprung;
  The fruit is dead, and yet the leaves be green;
My youth is gone, and yet I am but young;
  I saw the world, and yet I was not seen;
My thread is cut, and yet it is not spun;
And now I live, and now my life is done!

I sought my death, and found it in my womb;
  I looked for life, and saw it was a shade;
I trod the earth, and knew it was my tomb;
  And now I die, and now I am but made;
The glass is full, and now my glass is run;
And now I live, and now my life is done.

MADRIGAL

W. DRUMMOND

THIS Life, which seems so fair,
Is like a bubble blown up in the air
By sporting children's breath,
Who chase it everywhere
And strive who can most motion it bequeath;
And though it sometime seem of its own might
Like to an eye of gold to be fixed there,
And firm to hover in that empty height,
That only is because it is so light.
—But in that pomp it doth not long appear;
  For even when most admired, it in a thought,
  As swelled from nothing, doth dissolve in naught.

SPENSER TO MILTON

HENCE, ALL YOU VAIN DELIGHTS

J. FLETCHER

HENCE, all you vain delights,
As short as are the nights
  Wherein you spend your folly!
There 's naught in this life sweet,
If men were wise to see 't,
  But only melancholy—
  O sweetest melancholy!
Welcome, folded arms and fixèd eyes,
A sigh that piercing mortifies,
A look that 's fastened to the ground,
A tongue chained up without a sound!

Fountain-heads and pathless groves,
Places which pale passion loves!
Moonlight walks, when all the fowls
Are warmly housed save bats or owls!
  A midnight bell, a parting groan,
  These are the sounds we feed upon:
Then stretch our bones in a still gloomy valley;
Nothing 's so dainty sweet as lovely melancholy.

TO BLOSSOMS

R. HERRICK

FAIR pledges of a fruitful tree,
  Why do ye fall so fast?
  Your date is not so past
But you may stay yet here awhile
  To blush and gently smile,
      And go at last.

What! were ye born to be
  An hour or half's delight,
  And so to bid good night?

'Twas pity Nature brought you forth
  Merely to show your worth
    And lose you quite.

But you are lovely leaves, where we
  May read how soon things have
  Their end, though ne'er so brave :
And after they have shown their pride
  Like you awhile, they glide
    Into the grave.

TO MEADOWS

R. HERRICK

YE have been fresh and green,
  Ye have been filled with flowers,
And ye the walks have been
  Where maids have spent their hours.

You have beheld how they
  With wicker arks did come
To kiss and bear away
  The richer cowslips home.

You've heard them sweetly sing,
  And seen them in a round :
Each virgin like a spring,
  With honeysuckles crowned.

But now we see none here
  Whose silvery feet did tread
And with dishevelled hair
  Adorned this smoother mead.

Like unthrifts, having spent
  Your stock and needy grown,
You're left here to lament
  Your poor estates, alone.

YOU'VE HEARD THEM SWEETLY SING
AND SEEN THEM IN A ROUND

IN WESTMINSTER ABBEY

F. BEAUMONT

MORTALITY, behold and fear!
What a change of flesh is here!
Think how many royal bones
Sleep beneath this heap of stones!
Here they lie, had realms and lands,
Who now want strength to stir their hands:
Here from their pulpits sealed with dust
They preach, "In greatness is no trust."
Here is an acre sown indeed
With the richest, royallest seed
That the earth did e'er suck in
Since the first man died for sin:
Here the bones of birth have cried,
"Though gods they were, as men they died!"
Here are sands, ignoble things,
Dropt from the ruined sides of kings;
Here 's a world of pomp and state,
Buried in dust, once dead by fate.

THE NYMPH DESCRIBES HER FAWN

A. MARVELL

WITH sweetest milk and sugar first
I it at my own fingers nursed;
And as it grew, so every day
It waxed more white and sweet than they—
It had so sweet a breath! and oft
I blushed to see its foot more soft
And white,—shall I say,—than my hand?
Nay, any lady's of the land!

SPENSER TO MILTON

It is a wondrous thing how fleet
'Twas on those little silver feet:
With what a pretty skipping grace
It oft would challenge me the race:—
And when 't had left me far away
'Twould stay, and run again, and stay:
For it was nimbler much than hinds,
And trod as if on the four winds.

I have a garden of my own,
But so with roses overgrown
And lilies, that you would it guess
To be a little wilderness:
And all the spring-time of the year
It only lovèd to be there.
Among the beds of lilies I
Have sought it oft, where it should lie;
Yet could not, till itself would rise
Find it, although before mine eyes:—
For in the flaxen lilies' shade
It like a bank of lilies laid.

Upon the roses it would feed,
Until its lips e'en seem'd to bleed:
And then to me 'twould boldly trip,
And print those roses on my lip.
But all its chief delight was still
On roses thus itself to fill,
And its pure virgin limbs to fold
In whitest sheets of lilies cold:
Had it lived long, it would have been
Lilies without—roses within.

A LOVER'S LULLABY

G. GASCOIGNE

SING lullaby, as women do,
  Wherewith they bring their babes to rest;
And lullaby can I sing too,
  As womanly as can the best.
With lullaby they still the child;
And if I be not much beguiled,
Full many a wanton babe have I,
Which must be stilled with lullaby.

First lullaby my youthful years,
  It is now time to go to bed:
For crookèd age and hoary hairs
  Have won the haven within my head.
With lullaby, then, youth be still;
With lullaby content thy will;
Since courage quails and comes behind,
Go sleep, and so beguile thy mind!

Next lullaby my gazing eyes,
  Which wonted were to glance apace;
For every glass may now suffice
  To show the furrows in thy face.
With lullaby then wink awhile;
With lullaby your looks beguile;
Let no fair face, nor beauty bright,
Entice you oft with vain delight.

And lullaby my wanton will;
  Let reason's rule now reign thy thought;
Since all too late I find by skill
  How dear I have thy fancies bought;

With lullaby now take thine ease,
With lullaby thy doubts appease;
For trust to this, if thou be still,
My body shall obey thy will.

Thus lullaby my youth, mine eyes,
  My will, my ware, and all that was:
I can no more delays devise;
  But welcome pain, let pleasure pass.
With lullaby now take your leave;
With lullaby your dreams deceive;
And when you rise with waking eye,
Remember then this lullaby.

SHALL I COME, SWEET LOVE, TO THEE

T. CAMPION

SHALL I come, sweet Love, to thee
    When the evening beams are set?
Shall I not excluded be,
    Will you find no feignèd let?
Let me not, for pity, more
Tell the long hours at your door.

Who can tell what thief or foe,
    In the covert of the night,
For his prey will work my woe,
    Or through wicked foul despite?
So may I die unredrest
Ere my long love be possest.

But to let such dangers pass,
    Which a lover's thoughts disdain,
'Tis enough in such a place
    To attend love's joys in vain:
Do not mock me in thy bed,
While these cold nights freeze me dead.

SONNET

W. DRUMMOND

SLEEP, Silence' child, sweet father of soft rest,
Prince, whose approach peace to all mortals brings,
Indifferent host to shepherds and to kings,
Sole comforter of minds with grief opprest;
Lo, by thy charming rod all breathing things
Lie slumb'ring, with forgetfulness possest,
And yet o'er me to spread thy drowsy wings
Thou spares, alas! who cannot be thy guest.
Since I am thine, O come! but with that face
To inward light which thou art wont to show,
With feignèd solace ease a true-felt woe;
Or if, deaf god, thou do deny that grace,
Come as thou wilt, and what thou wilt bequeath,
I long to kiss the image of my death.

SONNET

SIR P. SIDNEY

COME, Sleep; O Sleep! the certain knot of peace,
The baiting-place of wit, the balm of woe,
The poor man's wealth, the prisoner's release,
Th' indifferent judge between the high and low;
With shield of proof shield me from out the prease
Of those fierce darts Despair at me doth throw:
O make in me those civil wars to cease;
I will good tribute pay, if thou do so.
Take thou of me smooth pillows, sweetest bed,
A chamber deaf of noise and blind of light,
A rosy garland and a weary head;
And if these things, as being thine by right,
Move not thy heavy grace, thou shalt in me
Livelier than elsewhere Stella's image see.

SLEEP, SILENCE' CHILD, SWEET FATHER OF SOFT REST
PRINCE, WHOSE APPROACH PEACE TO ALL MORTALS BRINGS

SPENSER TO MILTON

SONNET

W. SHAKESPEARE

FULL many a glorious morning have I seen
Flatter the mountain tops with sovereign eye,
Kissing with golden face the meadows green,
Gilding pale streams with heavenly alchemy;
Anon permit the basest clouds to ride
With ugly rack on his celestial face,
And from the forlorn world his visage hide,
Stealing unseen to west with this disgrace;
Even so my sun one early morn did shine
With all-triumphant splendour on my brow;
But out, alack! he was but one hour mine,
The region cloud hath masked him from me now.
Yet him for this my love no whit disdaineth;
Suns of the world may stain when heaven's sun staineth.

SONNET

W. SHAKESPEARE

THAT time of year thou mayst in me behold
When yellow leaves, or none, or few, do hang
Upon those boughs which shake against the cold,—
Bare ruined choirs where late the sweet birds sang.
In me thou see'st the twilight of such day
As after sunset fadeth in the west,
Which by and by black night doth take away,
Death's second self, that seals up all in rest.
In me thou see'st the glowing of such fire
That on the ashes of his youth doth lie,
As the death-bed whereon it must expire,
Consumed with that which it was nourished by:—
This thou perceiv'st, which makes thy love more strong,
To love that well which thou must leave ere long.

THE RETREAT

H. VAUGHAN

HAPPY those early days, when I
Shined in my Angel-infancy!
Before I understood this place
Appointed for my second race,
Or taught my soul to fancy aught
But a white, celestial thought;
When yet I had not walked above
A mile or two from my first Love,
And looking back, at that short space
Could see a glimpse of His bright face;
When on some gilded cloud or flower
My gazing soul would dwell an hour,
And in those weaker glories spy
Some shadows of eternity;
Before I taught my tongue to wound
My conscience with a sinful sound,
Or had the black art to dispense
A several sin to every sense,
But felt through all this fleshly dress
Bright shoots of everlastingness.
O how I long to travel back,
And tread again that ancient track!
That I might once more reach that plain
Where first I left my glorious train;
From whence th' enlightened spirit sees
That shady City of Palm trees!
But ah! my soul with too much stay
Is drunk, and staggers in the way:—
Some men a forward motion love,
But I by backward steps would move;
And when this dust falls to the urn,
In that state I came, return.

SPENSER TO MILTON

SONNET

M. DRAYTON

DEAR, why should you command me to my rest
When now the night doth summon all to sleep?
Methinks this time becometh lovers best;
Night was ordained together friends to keep.
How happy are all other living things
Which, though the day disjoin by several flight,
The quiet evening yet together brings,
And each returns unto his love at night!
O thou that else so courteous art to all,
Why shouldst thou, Night, abuse me only thus,
That every creature to his kind dost call,
And yet 'tis thou dost only sever us?
Well could I wish it would be ever day,
If when night comes you bid me go away.

SONNET

SIR P. SIDNEY

WITH how sad steps, O Moon, thou climb'st the skies!
How silently, and with how wan a face!
What! may it be that e'en in heavenly place
That busy Archer his sharp arrows tries?
Sure, if that long-with-love-acquainted eyes
Can judge of love, thou feel'st a lover's case:
I read it in thy looks; thy languished grace
To me, that feel the like, thy state descries.
Then, e'en of fellowship, O Moon, tell me,
Is constant love deemed there but want of wit?
Are beauties there as proud as here they be?
Do they above love to be loved, and yet
Those lovers scorn whom that love doth possess?
Do they call virtue there ungratefulness?

ENGLISH LYRICS

A LULLABY

ANON.

UPON my lap my sovereign sits
And sucks upon my breast ;
Meantime his love maintains my life
And gives my sense her rest.
  Sing lullaby, my little boy,
  Sing lullaby, mine only joy !

When thou hast taken thy repast,
Repose, my babe, on me ;
So may thy mother and thy nurse
Thy cradle also be.
  Sing lullaby, my little boy,
  Sing lullaby, mine only joy !

I grieve that duty doth not work
All that my wishing would ;
Because I would not be to thee
But in the best I should.
  Sing lullaby, my little boy,
  Sing lullaby, mine only joy !

Yet as I am, and as I may,
I must and will be thine,
Though all too little for thyself
Vouchsafing to be mine.
  Sing lullaby, my little boy,
  Sing lullaby, mine only joy !

SING LULLABY, MY LITTLE BOY
SING LULLABY, MINE ONLY JOY

SPENSER TO MILTON

WEEP NO MORE

J. FLETCHER

WEEP no more, nor sigh, nor groan ;
Sorrow calls no time that 's gone :
Violets plucked, the sweetest rain
Makes not fresh nor grow again ;
Trim thy locks, look cheerfully ;
Fate's hid ends eyes cannot see ;
Joy, as wingèd dreams flies past,
Why should sadness longer last ?
Grief is but a wound to woe ;
Gentlest fair, mourn, mourn no moe.

BLOW, BLOW, THOU WINTER WIND

W. SHAKESPEARE

BLOW, blow, thou winter wind,
Thou art not so unkind
    As man's ingratitude ;
Thy tooth is not so keen,
Because thou art not seen,
    Although thy breath be rude.
Heigh ho ! sing, heigh ho ! unto the green holly :
Most friendship is feigning, most loving mere folly :
    Then heigh ho, the holly :
    This life is most jolly.

Freeze, freeze, thou bitter sky,
Thou dost not bite so nigh
    As benefits forgot :
Though thou the waters warp,
Thy sting is not so sharp
    As friend remembered not.
Heigh ho ! sing, heigh ho ! unto the green holly :
Most friendship is feigning, most loving mere folly :
    Then heigh ho, the holly !
    This life is most jolly.

THE MAD MAID'S SONG

R. HERRICK

GOOD-MORROW to the day so fair,
  Good-morrow, sir, to you ;
Good-morrow to mine own torn hair
  Bedabbled with the dew.

Good-morning to this primrose too,
  Good-morrow to each maid
That will with flowers the tomb bestrew
  Wherein my love is laid.

Ah ! woe is me, woe, woe is me,
  Alack and well-a-day !
For pity, sir, find out that bee
  Which bore my love away.

I'll seek him in your bonnet brave,
  I'll seek him in your eyes ;
Nay, now I think they've made his grave
  I' th' bed of strawberries.

I'll seek him there ; I know ere this
  The cold, cold earth doth shake him ;
But I will go or send a kiss
  By you, sir, to awake him.

Pray hurt him not ; though he be dead,
  He knows well who do love him,
And who with green turfs rear his head,
  And who do rudely move him.

He 's soft and tender (pray take heed) ;
  With bands of cowslips bind him,
And bring him home ; but 'tis decreed
  That I shall never find him.

SONNET

W. SHAKESPEARE

WHEN in the chronicle of wasted time
I see descriptions of the fairest wights,
And beauty making beautiful old rhyme
In praise of ladies dead and lovely knights ;
Then, in the blazon of sweet beauty's best,
Of hand, of foot, of lip, of eye, of brow,
I see their antique pen would have expressed
Even such a beauty as you master now.
So all their praises are but prophecies
Of this our time, all you prefiguring ;
And for they looked but with divining eyes,
They had not skill enough your worth to sing :
For we, which now behold these present days,
Have eyes to wonder, but lack tongues to praise.

THE ANNIVERSARY

J. DONNE

ALL kings and all their favourites,—
All glory of honours, beauties, wits,—
The Sun itself, which makes times as they pass,
Is elder by a year now than it was
When thou and I first one another saw :—
All other things to their destruction draw ;
Only our love hath no decay :
This no to-morrow hath nor yesterday ;
Running it never runs from us away,
But truly keeps his first, last, everlasting day.

AWAY, DELIGHTS

J. FLETCHER

AWAY, delights ! go seek some other dwelling,
        For I must die.
Farewell, false love ! thy tongue is ever telling
        Lie after lie.
For ever let me rest now from thy smarts ;
        Alas, for pity go
        And fire their hearts
That have been hard to thee ! Mine was not so.

Never again deluding love shall know me,
        For I will die ;
And all those griefs, that think to overgrow me,
        Shall be as I :
For ever will I sleep, while poor maids cry—
        " Alas, for pity stay,
        And let us die
With thee ! Men cannot mock us in the clay."

SPENSER TO MILTON

COME, CHEERFUL DAY

T. CAMPION

COME, cheerful day, part of my life to me;
  For while thou view'st me with thy fading light
Part of my life doth still depart with thee,
  And I still onward haste to my last night:
Time's fatal wings do ever forward fly—
So every day we live a day we die.

But O ye nights, ordained for barren rest,
  How are my days deprived of life in you
When heavy sleep my soul hath dispossest,
  By feignèd death life sweetly to renew!
Part of my life, in that, you life deny:
So every day we live a day we die.

SONNET

W. SHAKESPEARE

LET me not to the marriage of true minds
Admit impediments. Love is not love
Which alters when it alteration finds,
Or bends with the remover to remove:
O, no! it is an ever-fixèd mark,
That looks on tempests and is never shaken;
It is the star to every wandering bark,
Whose worth 's unknown, although his height be taken.
Love 's not Time's fool, though rosy lips and cheeks
Within his bending sickle's compass come;
Love alters not with his brief hours and weeks,
But bears it out even to the edge of doom:—
If this be error and upon me proved,
I never writ, nor no man ever loved.

AT A SOLEMN MUSIC

J. MILTON

BLEST pair of Sirens, pledges of Heaven's joy,
Sphere-born harmonious sisters, Voice and Verse!
Wed your divine sounds, and mixed power employ,
Dead things with inbreathed sense able to pierce;
And to our high-raised phantasy present
That undisturbèd song of pure concent [1]
Aye sung before the sapphire-colour'd throne
        To Him that sits thereon,
With saintly shout and solemn jubilee;
Where the bright Seraphim in burning row
Their loud uplifted angel-trumpets blow;
And the Cherubic host in thousand quires
Touch their immortal harps of golden wires,
With those just Spirits that wear victorious palms,
        Hymns devout and holy psalms
        Singing everlastingly:
That we on Earth, with undiscording voice
May rightly answer that melodious noise;
As once we did, till disproportioned sin
Jarred against nature's chime, and with harsh din
Broke the fair music that all creatures made
To their great Lord, whose love their motion swayed
In perfect diapason, whilst they stood
In first obedience, and their state of good.
O may we soon again renew that song,
And keep in tune with Heaven, till God ere long
To His celestial consort us unite,
To live with Him, and sing in endless morn of light!

[1] Symphony.

SPENSER TO MILTON

THE WORLD

H. VAUGHAN

I saw Eternity the other night,
Like a great ring of pure and endless light,
All calm, as it was bright:—
And round beneath it, Time, in hours, days, years,
Driven by the spheres,
Like a vast shadow moved; in which the World
And all her train were hurled.

EARTHLY THINGS AND HEAVENLY

T. CAMPION

TO music bent is my retired mind
And fain would I some song of pleasure sing,
But in vain joys no comfort now I find;
From heavenly thoughts all true delight doth spring:
Thy power, O God, Thy mercies to record,
Will sweeten every note and every word.

All earthly pomp or beauty to express
Is but to carve in snow, on waves to write;
Celestial things, though men conceive them less,
Yet fullest are they in themselves of light:
Such beams they yield as know no means to die,
Such heat they cast as lifts the spirit high.

THE PROPHET

A. COWLEY

'TIS I who Love's Columbus am; 'tis I
Who must new worlds in it descry;
Rich worlds, that yield of treasure more
Than all that has been known before;
And yet, like his, I fear, my fate must be,
To find them out for others, not for me.

Me times to come, I know it, shall
Love's last and greatest Prophet call;
But, ah! what 's that if she refuse
To hear the wholesome doctrines of my Muse?
If to my share the Prophet's fate must come,
Hereafter fame, here martyrdom?

TO LUCASTA, ON GOING BEYOND THE SEAS

R. LOVELACE

IF to be absent were to be
Away from thee;
Or that when I am gone
You or I were alone;
Then, my Lucasta, might I crave
Pity from blustering wind, or swallowing wave.

But I'll not sigh one blast or gale
To swell my sail,
Or pay a tear to 'suage
The foaming blue-god's rage;
For whether he will let me pass
Or no, I'm still as happy as I was.

Though seas and land betwixt us both,
Our faith and troth,
Like separated souls,
All time and space controls:
Above the highest sphere we meet
Unseen, unknown, and greet as Angels greet.

So then we do anticipate
Our after-fate,
And are alive i' the skies,
If thus our lips and eyes
Can speak like spirits unconfined
In Heaven, their earthy bodies left behind.

SPENSER TO MILTON

A SONG

SIR J. SUCKLING

WHEN, dearest, I but think of thee
Methinks all things that lovely be
Are present, and my soul delighted;
For beauties that from worth arise
Are like the grace of deities,
Still present with us, though unsighted.

Thus whilst I sit, and sigh the day
With all his borrowed lights away,
Till night's black wings do overtake me,
Thinking on thee, thy beauties then,
As sudden lights do sleepy men,
So they by their bright rays awake me.

Thus absence dies, and dying proves
No absence can subsist with loves
That do partake of fair perfection;
Since in the darkest night they may,
By love's quick motion find a way
To see each other by reflection.

The waving sea can with each flood
Bathe some high promont that has stood
Far from the main up in the river.
Oh! think not then but love can do
As much, for that 's an ocean too,
Which flows not every day, but ever.

HIS MISTRESS'S FACE

T. CAMPION

AND would you see my Mistress' face?
It is a flowery garden place,
Where knots of beauty have such grace
That all is work and nowhere space.

It is a sweet delicious morn,
Where day is breeding, never born:
It is a meadow, yet unshorn,
Which thousand flowers do adorn.

It is the heaven's bright reflex,
Weak eyes to dazzle and to vex:
It is th' idea of her sex,
Envy of whom doth world perplex.

It is a face of death that smiles,
Pleasing, though it kill the whiles:
Where death and love in pretty wiles
Each other mutually beguiles.

It is fair beauty's freshest youth,
It is the feigned Elysium's truth:
The spring, that wintered hearts renew'th;
And this is that my soul pursu'th.

CASTARA

W. HABINGTON

LIKE the violet which alone
Prospers in some happy shade,
My Castara lives unknown,
To no looser eye betrayed.
  For she 's to herself untrue,
  Who delights in the public view.

Such is her beauty, as no arts
Have enriched with borrowed grace;
Her high birth no pride imparts,
For she blushes in her place.
  Folly boasts a glorious blood,
  She is noblest being good.

SPENSER TO MILTON

Cautious, she knew never yet
What a wanton courtship meant;
Nor speaks loud to boast her wit,
In her silence eloquent.
  Of herself survey she takes,
  But 'tween men no difference makes.

She her throne makes reason climb,
While wild passions captive lie;
And each article of time
Her pure thoughts to heaven fly;
  All her vows religious be,
  And her love she vows to me.

DISCOURSE WITH CUPID

BEN JONSON

NOBLEST Charis, you that are
Both my fortune and my star!
And do govern more my blood
Than the various moon the flood!
Hear, what late discourse of you
Love and I have had; and true.
'Mongst my muses finding me
Where he chanced your name to see
Set, and to this softer strain;
"Sure," said he, "if I have brain
This, here sung, can be no other
By description, but my mother!
So hath Homer praised her hair,
So Anacreon drawn the air
Of her face, and made to rise
Just about her sparkling eyes
Both her brows, bent like my bow;

By her looks I do her know,
Which you call my shafts. And see!
Such my mother's blushes be,
As the bath your verse discloses
In her cheeks, of milk and roses;
Such as oft I wanton in:
And, above her even chin,
Have you placed the bank of kisses,
Where, you say, men gather blisses,
Ripened with a breath more sweet
Than when flowers and west winds meet.
Nay, her white and polished neck
With the lace that doth it deck
Is my mother's! Hearts of slain
Lovers made into a chain!
And between each rising breast
Lies the valley, called my nest,
Where I sit and proyne my wings
After flight, and put new stings
To my shafts! Her very name
With my mother's is the same!"
I confess all, I replied,
And the glass hangs by her side,
And the girdle 'bout her waist,
All is Venus, save unchaste.
But, alas! thou seest the least
Of her good, who is the best
Of her sex; but could'st thou, Love,
Call to mind the forms that strove
For the apple, and those three
Make in one, the same were she;
For this beauty yet doth hide
Something more than thou hast spied.
Outward grace weak love beguiles;
She is Venus when she smiles,
But she 's Juno when she walks,
And Minerva when she talks.

ON A GIRDLE

E. WALLER

THAT which her slender waist confined
Shall now my joyful temples bind:
No monarch but would give his crown
His arms might do what this has done.

It was my Heaven's extremest sphere,
The pale which held that lovely deer:
My joy, my grief, my hope, my love
Did all within this circle move.

A narrow compass! and yet there
Dwelt all that 's good, and all that 's fair:
Give me but what this riband bound,
Take all the rest the Sun goes round.

A DEPOSITION FROM LOVE

T. CAREW

I WAS foretold, your rebel sex
Nor love nor pity knew,
And with what scorn you use to vex
Poor hearts that humbly sue ;
Yet I believed, to crown our pain,
Could we the fortress win,
The happy lover sure should gain
A paradise within ;
I thought Love's plagues like dragons sate
Only to fright us at the gate.

But I did enter, and enjoy
What happy lovers prove ;
For I could kiss, and sport, and toy,
And taste those sweets of love,
Which, had they but a lasting state,
Or if in Celia's breast
The force of love might not abate,
Jove were too mean a guest.
But now her breach of faith far more
Afflicts, than did her scorn before.

Hard fate ! to have been once possest,
As victor of a heart
Achieved with labour and unrest,
And then forced to depart.
If the stout foe will not resign
When I besiege a town,
I lose but what was never mine ;
But he that is cast down
From enjoyed beauty, feels a woe
Only deposèd kings can know.

SPENSER TO MILTON

SO SWEET IS THY DISCOURSE TO ME

T. CAMPION

So sweet is thy discourse to me,
  And so delightful is thy sight,
As I taste nothing right but thee:
  O why invented Nature light?
Was it alone for Beauty's sake
That her graced words might better take?

No more can I old joys recall,
  They now to me become unknown,
Not seeming to have been at all:
  Alas, how soon is this Love grown
To such a spreading height in me
As with it all must shadowed be!

THE CHRONICLE: A BALLAD

A. COWLEY

MARGARITA first possest,
If I remember well, my breast,
  Margarita first of all;
But when awhile the wanton maid
With my restless heart had played,
  Martha took the flying ball.

Martha soon did it resign
To the beauteous Catharine;
  Beauteous Catharine gave place
(Though loth and angry she to part
With the possession of my heart)
  To Eliza's conquering face.

Eliza till this hour might reign
Had she not evil counsels ta'en ;
  Fundamental laws she broke,
And still new favourites she chose,
Till up in arms my passions rose,
  And cast away her yoke.

Mary then, and gentle Anne,
Both to reign at once began ;
  Alternately they swayed,
And sometimes Mary was the fair,
And sometimes Anne the crown did wear,
  And sometimes both I obeyed.

Another Mary then arose,
And did rigorous laws impose ;
  A mighty tyrant she!
Long, alas! should I have been
Under that iron-sceptred queen,
  Had not Rebecca set me free.

When fair Rebecca set me free,
'Twas then a golden time with me.
  But soon those pleasures fled ;
For the gracious Princess died
In her youth and beauty's pride,
  And Judith reigned in her stead.

One month, three days, and half-an-hour
Judith held the sovereign power.
  Wondrous beautiful her face,
But so weak and small her wit
That she to govern was unfit,
  And so Susanna took her place.

But when Isabella came,
Armed with a resistless flame
  And th' artillery of her eye,
Whilst she proudly marched about
Greater conquests to find out,
  She beat out Susan by the by.

But in her place I then obeyed
Black-eyed Bess, her viceroy maid,
  To whom ensued a vacancy.
Thousand worst passions then possest
The interregnum of my breast ;
  Bless me from such an anarchy !

Gentle Henrietta then,
And a third Mary next began ;
  Then Joan, and Jane, and Audria ;
And then a pretty Thomasine,
And then another Catharine,
  And then a long et cætera.

But should I now to you relate
The strength and riches of their state,
  The powder, patches, and the pins,
The ribands, jewels, and the rings,
The lace, the paint, and warlike things
  That make up all their magazines ;

If I should tell the politic arts
To take and keep men's hearts,
  The letters, embassies, and spies,
The frowns, and smiles, and flatteries,
The quarrels, tears, and perjuries,
  Numberless, nameless mysteries !

And all the little lime-twigs laid
By Machiavel the waiting-maid;
  I more voluminous should grow
(Chiefly if I like them should tell
All change of weathers that befell)
  Than Hollinshed or Stow.

But I will briefer with them be,
Since few of them were long with me.
  An higher and a nobler strain
My present Emperess does claim,
Heleonora! first o' the name,
  Whom God grant long to reign!

OUT UPON IT, I HAVE LOVED

SIR J. SUCKLING

OUT upon it, I have loved
Three whole days together;
And am like to love three more,
If it prove fair weather.

Time shall moult away his wings
E'er he shall discover
In the whole wide world again
Such a constant lover.

But the spite on 't is, no praise
Is due at all to me.
Love with me had made no stays
Had it any been but she.

Had it any been but she,
And that very face,
There had been at least ere this
A dozen dozen in her place.

SPENSER TO MILTON

SWEET LOVE, MY ONLY TREASURE

ANON.

SWEET Love, my only treasure,
For service long unfeigned,
Wherein I nought have gained,
Vouchsafe this little pleasure,
    To tell me in what part
    My lady keeps my heart.

If in her hair so slender,
Like golden nets entwined,
Which fire and art have 'fined,
Her thrall my heart I render
    For ever to abide
    With locks so dainty tied.

If in her eyes she binds it,
Wherein that fire was framed
By which it is enflamed,
I dare not look to find it;
    I only wish it sight
    To see that pleasant light.

But if her breast have deignèd
With kindness to receive it,
I am content to leave it,
Though death thereby were gainèd;
    Then, Lady, take your own,
    That lives by you alone.

TO DAISIES

R. HERRICK

SHUT not so soon! the dull-eyed Night
   Has not as yet begun
To make a seizure on the light,
   Or to seal up the sun.

No marigolds yet closèd are,
   No shadows great appear;
Nor doth the early shepherd's star
   Shine like a spangle here.

Stay but until my Julia close
   Her life-begetting eye;
And let the whole world then dispose
   Itself to live or die.

THE NIGHT-PIECE: TO JULIA

R. HERRICK

HER eyes the glow-worm lend thee,
The shooting stars attend thee;
      And the elves also,
      Whose little eyes glow
Like the sparks of fire, befriend thee.

No Will-o'-the-wisp mislight thee,
Nor snake nor slow-worm bite thee;
      But on, on thy way
      Not making a stay,
Since ghost there 's none to affright thee.

SPENSER TO MILTON

Let not the dark thee cumber:
What though the moon does slumber?
    The stars of the night
    Will lend thee their light
Like tapers clear without number.

Then, Julia, let me woo thee,
Thus, thus to come unto me;
    And when I shall meet
    Thy silvery feet
My soul I'll pour into thee.

TO DIANEME

R. HERRICK

SWEET, be not proud of those two eyes
Which starlike sparkle in their skies;
Nor be you proud that you can see
All hearts your captives, yours yet free;
Be you not proud of that rich hair
Which wantons with the love-sick air;
Whenas that ruby which you wear,
Sunk from the tip of your soft ear,
Will last to be a precious stone
When all your world of beauty 's gone.

RESOLVED TO LOVE

A. COWLEY

I WONDER what the grave and wise
  Think of all us that love;
Whether our pretty fooleries
  Their mirth or anger move;
They understand not breath that words does want;
Our sighs to them are insignificant.

One of them saw me th' other day
  Touch the dear hand which I admire,
My soul was melting straight away,
  And dropped before the fire.
This silly wise man, who pretends to know,
Asked why I looked so pale, and trembled so?

Another from my mistress' door
  Saw me with eyes all wat'ry come,
Nor could the hidden cause explore,
  But thought some smoke was in the room:
Such ignorance from unwounded learning came,
He knew tears made by smoke, but not by flame.

If learned in other things you be,
  And have in love no skill,
For God's sake keep your arts from me,
  For I'll be ignorant still.
Study or action others may embrace,
My love's my business, and my books her face.

SPENSER TO MILTON

TO MY YOUNG LADY LUCY SIDNEY

E. WALLER

WHY came I so untimely forth
  Into a world which, wanting thee,
Could entertain us with no worth
  Or shadow of felicity,
That time should me so far remove
From that which I was born to love?

Yet, Fairest Blossom, do not slight
  That age which you may know so soon,
The rosy morn resigns her light
  And milder glory to the noon;
And then what wonders shall you do
Whose dawning beauty warms us so!

Hope waits upon the flowery prime,
  And Summer, though it be less gay,
Yet is not looked on as a time
  Of declination or decay:
For with a full hand that does bring
All that was promised by the Spring.

TO A VERY YOUNG LADY

SIR C. SEDLEY

AH, Chloris! could I now but sit
  As unconcerned as when
Your infant beauty could beget
  No happiness or pain!
When I the dawn used to admire,
  And praised the coming day,
I little thought the rising fire
  Would take my rest away.

Your charms in harmless childhood lay
  Like metals in the mine;
Age from no face takes more away
  That youth concealed in thine.
But as your charms insensibly
  To their perfection prest,
So Love as unperceived did fly,
  And centred in my breast.

My passion with your beauty grew,
  While Cupid at my heart,
Still as his mother favoured you,
  Threw a new flaming dart:
Each gloried in their wanton part;
  To make a lover, he
Employed the utmost of his art—
  To make a Beauty, she.

LOVE IN HER SUNNY EYES

A. COWLEY

LOVE in her sunny eyes does basking play;
Love walks the pleasant mazes of her hair;
Love does on both her lips for ever stray,
And sows and reaps a thousand kisses there.

SPENSER TO MILTON

DELIGHT IN DISORDER

R. HERRICK

A SWEET disorder in the dress
Kindles in clothes a wantonness:
A lawn about the shoulders thrown
Into a fine distraction,
An erring lace, which here and there
Enthrals the crimson stomacher,
A cuff neglectful, and thereby
Ribbons to flow confusedly;
A winning wave, deserving note,
In the tempestuous petticoat;
A careless shoe-string, in whose tie
I see a wild civility;—
Do more bewitch me, than when art
Is too precise in every part.

SONG

B. JONSON

STILL to be neat, still to be drest
As you were going to a feast;
Still to be powdered, still perfumed:
Lady, it is to be presumed,
Though art's hid causes are not found,
All is not sweet, all is not sound.

Give me a look, give me a face
That makes simplicity a grace;
Robes loosely flowing, hair as free:
Such sweet neglect more taketh me
Than all th' adulteries of art;
They strike mine eyes, but not my heart.

MADRIGAL

ANON.

LOVE not me for comely grace,
For my pleasing eye or face,
Nor for any outward part,
No, nor for a constant heart:
For these may fail or turn to ill,
So thou and I shall sever:
Keep, therefore, a true woman's eye,
And love me still but know not why—
So hast thou the same reason still
To dote upon me ever!

UPON JULIA'S CLOTHES

R. HERRICK

WHENAS in silks my Julia goes,
Then, then, methinks, how sweetly flows
The liquefaction of her clothes!

Next, when I cast mine eyes and see
That brave vibration each way free,
—O how that glittering taketh me!

SEE WHERE MY LOVE A-MAYING GOES

ANON.

SEE where my love a-maying goes,
With sweet dame Flora sporting!
She most alone with nightingales
In woods delights consorting.
Turn again, my dearest!
The pleasant'st air 's in meadows:
Else by the rivers let us breathe,
And kiss amongst the willows.

SEE WHERE MY LOVE A-MAYING GOES,
WITH SWEET DAME FLORA SPORTING

SPENSER TO MILTON

TO ANTHEA, WHO MAY COMMAND HIM ANYTHING

R. HERRICK

BID me to live, and I will live
  Thy Protestant to be,
Or bid me love, and I will give
  A loving heart to thee.

A heart as soft, a heart as kind,
  A heart as sound and free
As in the whole world thou canst find,
  That heart I'll give to thee.

Bid that heart stay, and it will stay
  To honour thy decree:
Or bid it languish quite away,
  And 't shall do so for thee.

Bid me to weep, and I will weep
  While I have eyes to see:
And, having none, yet will I keep
  A heart to weep for thee.

Bid me despair, and I'll despair
  Under that cypress-tree:
Or bid me die, and I will dare
  E'en death to die for thee.

Thou art my life, my love, my heart,
  The very eyes of me:
And hast command of every part
  To live and die for thee.

LOVE'S SPRING

R. CRASHAW

THOUGH now 'tis neither May nor June,
And nightingales are out of tune,
Yet in these leaves, fair One, there lies—
Sworn servant to your sweetest eyes—
A nightingale, who, may she spread
In your white bosom her chaste bed,
Spite of all the maiden snow
Those pure untrodden paths can show,
You straight shall see her wake and rise,
Taking fresh life from your fair eyes,
And with claspt wings proclaim a Spring,
Where Love and she shall sit and sing;
For lodged so near your sweetest throat
What nightingale can lose her note?
Nor let her kindred birds complain
Because she breaks the year's old reign;
For let them know she 's none of those
Hedge-quiristers whose music owes
Only such strains as serve to keep
Sad shades, and sing dull night asleep.
No, she 's a priestess of that grove,
The holy chapel of chaste love,
Your virgin bosom. Then whate'er
Poor laws divide the public year,
Whose revolutions wait upon
The wild turns of the wanton sun,
Be you the Lady of Love's year.
Where your eyes shine his suns appear;
There all the year is Love's long Spring,
There all the year
Love's nightingales shall sit and sing.

SPENSER TO MILTON

TO LAURA

T. CAMPION

ROSE-CHEEKED Laura, come!
Sing thou smoothly with thy beauty's
Silent music, either other
Sweetly gracing.

Lovely forms do flow
From concent divinely framed,
Heaven is music, and thy beauty's
Birth is heavenly.

These dull notes we sing
Discords need for helps to grace them;
Only beauty purely loving
Knows no discord;

But still moves delight,
Like clear springs renewed by flowing
Ever perfect, ever in them-
selves eternal.

TURN BACK, YOU WANTON FLYER

T. CAMPION

TURN back, you wanton flyer,
And answer my desire
With mutual greeting.
Yet bend a little nearer,—
True beauty still shines clearer
In closer meeting.
Hearts with hearts delighted
Should strive to be united
Each other's arms with arms enchaining:
Hearts with a thought,
Rosy lips with a kiss still entertaining.

What harvest half so sweet is
As still to reap the kisses
    Grown ripe in sowing?
And straight to be receiver
Of that which thou art giver,
    Rich in bestowing?
There 's no strict observing
Of times' or seasons' swerving,
    There is ever one fresh spring abiding;
Then what we sow with our lips
    Let us reap, love's gains dividing.

A PEDLAR'S SONG

W. SHAKESPEARE

LAWN as white as driven snow;
Cypress black as e'er was crow;
Gloves as sweet as damask roses;
Masks for faces and for noses;
Bugle bracelet, necklace amber,
Perfume for a lady's chamber;
Golden quoifs and stomachers,
For my lads to give their dears:
Pins and poking-sticks of steel,
What maids lack from head to heel:
Come buy of me, come; come buy, come buy;
Buy, lads, or else your lasses cry:
    Come buy.

SPENSER TO MILTON

A SHEPHERD'S PLAINT

W. BROWNE

So shuts the marigold her leaves
  At the departure of the sun;
So from the honeysuckle sheaves
  The bee goes when the day is done;
So sits the turtle when she is but one,
And so all woe, as I since she is gone.

To some few birds kind Nature hath
  Made all the summer as one day:
Which once enjoyed, cold winter's wrath
  As night they sleeping pass away.
Those happy creatures are, they know not yet
The pain to be deprived, or to forget.

I oft have heard men say there be
  Some that with confidence profess
The helpful Art of Memory:
  But could they teach forgetfulness,
I'd learn, and try what further art could do
To make me love her and forget her too.

Sad melancholy, that persuades
  Men from themselves, to think they be
Headless, or other bodies shades,
  Hath long and bootless dwelt with me.
For could I think She some idea were,
I still might love, forget, and have her here.

SONG

W. SHAKESPEARE

FEAR no more the heat o' the sun,
  Nor the furious winter's rages;
Thou thy worldly task hast done,
  Home art gone, and ta'en thy wages:
Golden lads and girls all must,
As chimney-sweepers, come to dust.

Fear no more the frown o' the great,
  Thou art past the tyrant's stroke;
Care no more to clothe and eat;
  To thee the reed is as the oak:
The sceptre, learning, physic, must
All follow this, and come to dust.

Fear no more the lightning-flash,
  Nor the all-dreaded thunder-stone;
Fear not slander, censure rash;
  Thou hast finished joy and moan:
All lovers young, all lovers must
Consign to thee, and come to dust.

No exorciser harm thee!
Nor no witchcraft charm thee!
Ghost unlaid forbear thee!
Nothing ill come near thee!
Quiet consummation have;
And renownèd be thy grave!

SPENSER TO MILTON

SONNET

SIR P. SIDNEY

LEAVE me, O Love, which reachest but to dust;
And thou, my mind, aspire to higher things;
Grow rich in that which never taketh rust;
Whatever fades but fading pleasure brings.
Draw in thy beams and humble all thy might
To that sweet yoke where lasting freedoms be;
Which breaks the clouds, and opens forth the light,
That doth both shine, and give us sight to see.
Oh, take fast hold; let that light be thy guide
In this small course which birth draws out to death,
And think how ill becometh him to slide
Who seeketh heaven and comes of heavenly breath.
Then farewell, world! thy uttermost I see;
Eternal Love, maintain thy life in me!

ON HIS BLINDNESS

J. MILTON

WHEN I consider how my light is spent
Ere half my days, in this dark world and wide,
And that one talent which is death to hide
Lodged with me useless, though my soul more bent
To serve therewith my Maker, and present
My true account, lest He returning chide,—
Doth God exact day-labour, light denied?
I fondly ask:—But Patience, to prevent
That murmur, soon replies; God doth not need
Either man's work, or His own gifts: who best
Bear His mild yoke, they serve Him best: His state
Is kingly; thousands at His bidding speed
And post o'er land and ocean without rest:—
They also serve who only stand and wait.

ENGLISH LYRICS

A LAND DIRGE

J. WEBSTER

CALL for the robin-redbreast and the wren,
Since o'er shady groves they hover,
And with leaves and flowers do cover
The friendless bodies of unburied men.
Call unto his funeral dole
The ant, the field-mouse, and the mole,
To rear him hillocks that shall keep him warm,
And (when gay tombs are robbed) sustain no harm ;
But keep the wolf far hence, that's foe to men
For with his nails he'll dig them up again.

ARIEL'S SONG

W. SHAKESPEARE

FULL fathom five thy father lies ;
  Of his bones are coral made ;
Those are pearls that were his eyes :
  Nothing of him that doth fade,
But doth suffer a sea-change
Into something rich and strange.
Sea-nymphs hourly ring his knell :
                    Ding-dong.
  Hark ! now I hear them,—
            Ding-dong, bell !

FULL FATHOM FIVE THY FATHER LIES

SPENSER TO MILTON

ON THE LATE MASSACRE IN PIEDMONT

J. MILTON

AVENGE, O Lord! Thy slaughtered saints, whose bones
Lie scattered on the Alpine mountains cold;
Even them who kept Thy truth so pure of old
When all our fathers worshipped stocks and stones
Forget not: In Thy book record their groans
Who were Thy sheep, and in their ancient fold
Slain by the bloody Piemontese, that rolled
Mother with infant down the rocks. Their moans
The vales redoubled to the hills, and they
To Heaven. Their martyr'd blood and ashes sow
O'er all the Italian fields, where still doth sway
The triple Tyrant: that from these may grow
A hundred-fold, who, having learnt Thy way,
Early may fly the Babylonian woe.

ASPATIA'S SONG

J. FLETCHER

LAY a garland on my hearse
  Of the dismal yew;
Maidens, willow branches bear;
  Say, I died true.

My love was false, but I was firm
  From my hour of birth.
Upon my buried body lie
  Lightly, gentle earth!

CRABBED AGE AND YOUTH

W. SHAKESPEARE

CRABBED Age and Youth
Cannot live together:
Youth is full of pleasance,
Age is full of care;
Youth like summer morn,
Age like winter weather;
Youth like summer brave,
Age like winter bare.
Youth is full of sport,
Age's breath is short;
Youth is nimble, Age is lame;
Youth is hot and bold,
Age is weak and cold;
Youth is wild, and Age is tame.
Age, I do abhor thee;
Youth, I do adore thee;
O, my Love, my Love is young!
Age, I do defy thee:
O, sweet shepherd, hie thee!
For methinks thou stay'st too long.

TO ECHO

J. MILTON

SWEET Echo, sweetest nymph, that liv'st unseen
        Within thy airy shell,
    By slow Meander's margent green,
And in the violet-embroider'd vale,
        Where the love-lorn nightingale
Nightly to thee her sad song mourneth well;
Canst thou not tell me of a gentle pair
        That likest thy Narcissus are?
        O, if thou have
    Hid them in some flowery cave,
        Tell me but where,
    Sweet queen of parley, daughter of the sphere!
    So may'st thou be translated to the skies,
And give resounding grace to all Heaven's harmonies.

SONG OF THE EMIGRANTS IN BERMUDA

A. MARVELL

WHERE the remote Bermudas ride
In the ocean's bosom unespied,
From a small boat that rowed along
The listening winds received this song.
"What should we do but sing His praise
That led us through the watery maze
Where He the huge sea-monsters wracks,
That lift the deep upon their backs,
Unto an isle so long unknown,
And yet far kinder than our own?
He lands us on a grassy stage,
Safe from the storms, and prelate's rage:
He gave us this eternal Spring
Which here enamels everything,
And sends the fowls to us in care
On daily visits through the air,
He hangs in shades the orange bright
Like golden lamps in a green night,
And does in the pomegranates close
Jewels more rich than Ormus shows:
He makes the figs our mouths to meet
And throws the melons at our feet;
But apples plants of such a price,
No tree could ever bear them twice.
With cedars chosen by His hand
From Lebanon He stores the land;
And makes the hollow seas that roar
Proclaim the ambergris on shore.
He cast (of which we rather boast)
The Gospel's pearl upon our coast;
And in these rocks for us did frame
A temple where to sound His name.

Oh ! let our voice His praise exalt
Till it arrive at Heaven's vault,
Which thence (perhaps) rebounding may
Echo beyond the Mexique bay ! "
—Thus sung they in the English boat
A holy and a cheerful note :
And all the way, to guide their chime,
With falling oars they kept the time.

THE PILGRIMAGE

SIR W. RALEIGH

GIVE me my scallop-shell of quiet,
  My staff of faith to walk upon,
My scrip of joy, immortal diet,
  My bottle of salvation,
My gown of glory, hope's true gage ;
And thus I'll take my pilgrimage.

Blood must be my body's balmer ;
  No other balm will there be given ;
Whilst my soul, like quiet palmer,
  Travelleth towards the land of heaven ;
Over the silver mountains,
Where spring the nectar fountains :
    There will I kiss
    The bowl of bliss ;
And drink mine everlasting fill
Upon every milken hill.
My soul will be a-dry before ;
But after, it will thirst no more.

ENGLISH LYRICS

THE WHITE ISLAND

R. HERRICK

In this world, the Isle of Dreams,
While we sit by sorrow's streams,
Tears and terror are our themes
Reciting:

But when once from hence we fly,
More and more approaching nigh
Unto young Eternity
Uniting:

In that whiter island, where
Things are evermore sincere;
Candour here, and lustre there
Delighting:

—There no monstrous fancies shall
Out of Hell an horror call,
To create (or cause at all)
Affrighting.

There in calm and cooling sleep
We our eyes shall never steep;
But eternal watch shall keep
Attending
Pleasures such as shall pursue
Me immortalized, and you;
And fresh joys, as never too
Have ending.

SPENSER TO MILTON

THE LOWEST TREES HAVE TOPS

ANON.

THE lowest trees have tops, the ant her gall,
The fly her spleen, the little spark his heat;
And slender hairs cast shadows, though but small,
And bees have stings, although they be not great;
Seas have their source, and so have shallow springs;
And love is love, in beggars and in kings!

Where waters smoothest run, deep are the fords;
The dial stirs, yet none perceives it move;
The firmest faith is in the fewest words;
The turtles cannot sing, and yet they love;
True hearts have eyes and ears, no tongues to speak;
They hear, and see, and sigh, and then they break!

FRIENDS IN PARADISE

H. VAUGHAN

THEY are all gone into the world of light!
And I alone sit lingering here;
Their very memory is fair and bright,
And my sad thoughts doth clear:

It glows and glitters in my cloudy breast,
Like stars upon some gloomy grove,
Or those faint beams in which this hill is drest,
After the sun's remove.

I see them walking in an air of glory,
Whose light doth trample on my days:
My days, which are at best but dull and hoary,
Mere glimmering and decays.

O holy Hope! and high Humility,
    High as the heavens above!
These are your walks, and you have shewed them me,
        To kindle my cold love.

Dear, beauteous Death! the jewel of the just,
    Shining no where, but in the dark;
What mysteries do lie beyond thy dust,
        Could man outlook that mark!

He that hath found some fledged bird's nest, may know
    At first sight, if the bird be flown;
But what fair dell or grove he sings in now,
        That is to him unknown.

And yet, as Angels in some brighter dreams
    Call to the soul, when man doth sleep;
So some strange thoughts transcend our wonted themes,
        And into glory peep.

SONNET

E. SPENSER

MOST glorious Lord of Life, that on this day
Didst make Thy triumph over death and sin,
And having harrowed hell, didst bring away
Captivity thence captive, us to win:
This joyous day, dear Lord, with joy begin,
And grant that we, for whom thou diddest die,
Being with Thy dear blood clean washed from sin,
May live for ever in felicity!
And that Thy love we weighing worthily,
May likewise love Thee for the same again;
And for Thy sake, that all like dear didst buy,
With love may one another entertain.
So let us love, dear Love, like as we ought,
—Love is the lesson which the Lord us taught.

SPENSER TO MILTON

THE BURNING BABE

R. SOUTHWELL

As I in hoary winter's night
  Stood shivering in the snow,
Surprised was I with sudden heat
  Which made my heart to glow;
And lifting up a fearful eye
  To view what fire was near,
A pretty babe all burning bright
  Did in the air appear;
Who, scorchèd with excessive heat,
  Such floods of tears did shed
As though His floods should quench His flames,
  Which with His tears were fed:
"Alas!" quoth He, "but newly born
  In fiery heats I fry,
Yet none approach to warm their hearts
  Or feel my fire but I!

"My faultless breast the furnace is;
  The fuel, wounding thorns;
Love is the fire, and sighs the smoke;
  The ashes, shames and scorns;
The fuel Justice layeth on,
  And Mercy blows the coals,
The metal in this furnace wrought
  Are men's defilèd souls:
For which, as now on fire I am
  To work them to their good,
So will I melt into a bath,
  To wash them in my blood."
With this He vanished out of sight
  And swiftly shrunk away,
And straight I callèd unto mind
  That it was Christmas Day.

AN EPITAPH UPON HUSBAND AND WIFE WHO DIED AND WERE BURIED TOGETHER

R. CRASHAW

To these whom Death again did wed
This grave 's their second marriage bed,
For though the hand of Fate could force
'Twixt soul and body a divorce,
It could not sunder man and wife,
'Cause they both livèd but one life.
Peace, good reader, do not weep;
Peace, the lovers are asleep.
They, sweet turtles, folded lie
In the last knot love could tie,
And though they lie as they were dead,
Their pillow stone, their sheets of lead,—
Pillow hard and sheets not warm,—
Love made the bed, they'll take no harm.
Let them sleep, let them sleep on,
Till this stormy night be gone,
And th' eternal morrow dawn;
Then the curtain will be drawn,
And they wake into that light
Whose day shall never die in night.

DEATH THE LEVELLER

J. SHIRLEY

The glories of our blood and state
  Are shadows, not substantial things;
There is no armour against Fate;
  Death lays his icy hand on kings:
    Sceptre and Crown
    Must tumble down,

And in the dust be equal made
With the poor crookèd scythe and spade.

Some men with swords may reap the field,
And plant fresh laurels where they kill:
But their strong nerves at last must yield;
They tame but one another still:
Early or late
They stoop to fate,
And must give up their murmuring breath
When they, pale captives, creep to death.

The garlands wither on your brow;
Then boast no more your mighty deeds;
Upon Death's purple altar now
See where the victor-victim bleeds.
Your heads must come
To the cold tomb:
Only the actions of the just
Smell sweet and blossom in their dust.

THE PULLEY

G. HERBERT

WHEN God at first made Man,
Having a glass of blessings standing by,—
Let us, said He, pour on him all we can;
Let the world's riches which dispersèd lie
Contract into a span.

So strength first made a way,
Then beauty flowed, then wisdom, honour, pleasure:
When almost all was out, God made a stay,
Perceiving that, alone of all his treasure,
Rest in the bottom lay.

For if I should, said He,
Bestow this jewel also on My creature,
He would adore My gifts instead of Me,
And rest in Nature, not the God of Nature:
So both should losers be.

Yet let him keep the rest,
But keep them with repining restlessness;
Let him be rich and weary, that at least,
If goodness lead him not, yet weariness
May toss him to My breast.

CLOSE NOW THINE EYES

F. QUARLES

CLOSE now thine eyes and rest secure;
Thy soul is safe enough; thy body sure;
He that loves thee, He that keeps
And guards thee never slumbers, never sleeps.
The smiling Conscience in a sleeping breast
Has only peace, has only rest;
The music and the mirth of kings
Are all but very discords when she sings.
Then close thine eyes and rest secure;
No sleep so sweet as thine, no rest so sure.

FINIS

INDEX OF AUTHORS

INDEX OF FIRST LINES

INDEX OF FIRST LINES

ENGLISH LYRICS

INDEX OF FIRST LINES